The Way:
Out of Self-Sabotage; Into Self-Mastery

By Hunter Michael Charneski

Soaring Beyond, an imprint of Winged Publications

ISBN: 978-1-965352-14-4

Dedication

To my wife, Tiffany. Though this book was written for today's Self-Sabotaging Man, behind him is a Tiffany, Cassandra, Liz, or Toni of his own—and she isn't giving up on him. She's telling him the same thing you told me when I was at my lowest: "I can't wait till the day you see how incredible you really are." Without you, Tiffany, I never would have made it to that day. But I did. This book is literal proof of that.

I love you.

The Way:
Out of Self-Sabotage; Into Self-Mastery
By Hunter Michael Charneski

Contents

Dedication v
Acknowledgments i
What I Know—Part One 7
The Way—Part One 9
What I Know—Part Two 10
What I Know—Part Three 22
PART ONE: DEFINING DEFAULT 28
The Victim and The Villain—Part One 29
The Victim and The Villain—Part Two 33
The Victim and The Villain—Part Three 35
SECTION II: DEFAULT AND SELF-SABOTAGE 39
Default and the Daimon—Part One 41
Default and the Daimon—Part Two 43
Default and Handsaws 45
Default and Wanderers 47
Default and the Disease of More—Part One 49
Default Is Environmental 51
Default Is Mental, Too 53
Default and Better Parents 55
Default and Life's Burn Pile 57
Default Is Cyclical 59

Default and Shadow Careers 63
Default and Antibiotics 65
Default and Lifelong Caterpillars 67
Default Is a Judge 69
Default Doesn't Care 71
Default's Gateway Drug 73
Default and Going All-In 77
Default and Problems—Part One 79
Default and Problems—Part Two 81
Default and Story—Part One 83
Default Is a Hydra 85
Default and Outliers 87
Default, Idols, and God 89
A New Default—Part One 93
SECTION III: MY DEFAULT 95
Default, Families, and Lies 97
Default and "No" 101
Default and "Love" 103
Default and Story—Part Two 105
The Beginning of the End 107
The Way—Part Two 109
The Way—Part Three 111
Default and Addiction—Part One 113
Default and Addiction—Part Two 115
Be a Grimit—Part One 117
Default and Transformation 121

Self-Sabotage on Steroids 123
#SPRINTORDIE—Part One 127
The Way—Part Four 129
This Isn't Fun Anymore 133
#SPRINTORDIE—Part Two 137
Necessary Failure 139
Paying It Backward—Part One 141
The Letter 145
More Than Okay 151
Write Your Book 153
Being a Family 155
Self-Realization—Part One 156
Be a Grimit—Part Two 159
The Disease of More—Part Two 161
The Kiss of Death 163
Not This Year 165
A New Default—Part Two 169
PART TWO: REDEFINING DEFAULT 171
60. Overture 173
SECTION I: THE CALL TO ADVENTURE 177
A Quantum Leap 179
SECTION II: REFUSAL OF THE CALL 185
Next 187
SECTION III: SUPERNATURAL AID 189
The Billion Dollar Idea 191
A Worthy Investment—Part One 195

SECTION IV: CROSSING THE FIRST THRESHOLD ... 197
Put God First—Part One ... 199
The Seminar ... 201
The Way—Part Five ... 205
SECTION V: BELLY OF THE WHALE ... 209
The Chairman ... 211
SECTION VI: ROAD OF TRIALS ... 215
The Golden Calf—Part One ... 217
Change Your Story—Part One ... 219
The Golden Calf—Part Two ... 221
Change Your Story—Part Two ... 225
Starving—Part One ... 227
Starving—Part Two ... 231
Go All-In—Part One ... 235
Go All-In—Part Two ... 238
Change Your Story—Part Three ... 241
SECTION VII: MEETING WITH THE GODDESS ... 243
What Every Story Needs ... 245
SECTION VIII: TEMPTATION ... 247
Run *Your* Race—Part One ... 249
Run *Your* Race—Part Two ... 251
The Golden Calf—Part Three ... 253
SECTION IX: ATONEMENT WITH THE FATHER ... 257
Change Your Story—Part Four ... 259
The Golden Calf—Part Four ... 261
The Golden Calf—Part Five ... 263

Who Are You More Afraid to Lose? 267
Self-Realization—Part Two 269
SECTION X: THE ALL IS LOST MOMENT 273
Self-Realization—Part Three 275
My All is Lost Moment 277
SECTION XI: THE EPIPHANAL MOMENT 279
Self-Mastery 281
SECTION XII: REFUSAL OF THE RETURN 283
After the Wilderness 285
SECTION XIII: MAGIC FLIGHT 289
Motivated Sellers 291
SECTION XIV: RESCUE FROM WITHOUT 293
An Act of God 295
SECTION XV: A GIFT FOR THE PEOPLE 299
Put God First—Part Two 301
SECTION XVI: MASTER OF TWO WORLDS 303
Do What You Do Best 305
SECTION XVII: FREEDOM TO LIVE 309
The Way—Part Six 311
PART THREE: SELF-MASTERY 315
SECTION I: WHAT IS SELF-MASTERY? 317
What is Self-Mastery?—Part One 319
What is Self-Mastery?—Part Two 321
What is Self-Mastery?—Part Three 323
Get Your Act Together 325
Hedgehogs 327

Gold in the Dirt 329
Fly—Part One 331
Fly—Part Two 333
Be All You Can Be—Part One 335
Be All You Can Be—Part Two 337
Be All You Can Be—Part Three 339
Be All You Can Be—Part Four 341
Empathy and Connection—Part One 343
Empathy and Connection—Part Two 345
A Different Game—Part One 347
A Different Game—Part Two 349
Self-Mastery and Fear 351
SECTION II: OFF THE SCRIPT 353
Off the Script—Part One 355
Off the Script—Part Two 357
Here's How it Works 359
Put God First—Part Three 361
Go All-In—Part Three 365
Run *Your* Race—Part Three 369
Gravity 373
SECTION III: SCRATCH YOUR OWN ITCH 377
Scratch Your Own Itch—Part One 379
Let It Go 381
Done > Perfect 383
How to Finish—Part One 385
How to Finish—Part Two 387

Paying It Backward—Part Two 389
Artistic Warriors—Part One 391
Artistic Warriors—Part Two 393
A Worthy Investment—Part Two 395
A New Default—Part Two...397
Subway and The Way 399
Why the 400?..403
Scratch Your Own Itch—Part Two................................405
Scratch Your Own Itch—Part Three 407
Coda 409

Acknowledgments

Thank you to my Lord and Savior, Jesus Christ.

To my son, Sam, thank you for being so patient with me.

Thank you to my mother, Shelly. God, what a gal.

To the man who's always wanted to be my dad, Andy Hilliard, I say: "Thanks dad."

Thank you to my fifth-grade teacher, Mrs. Schmitz, you were the catalyst for me becoming a writer when I was an eleven-year-old kid.

Thanks to my friend, Kyle Galik. *Friend* is a misnomer, you're my brother. Blood wouldn't make us any closer.

To Kyle's dad, Bill, the only other person I've felt comfortable enough calling *Dad* besides Andy and my biological father. I can't wait for you to read this book. It's basically a 50K word thank you to *you.* So, thank you.

Thank you to my defensive line coach at St. Cloud State, Steve Grimit. It's cliché, I know, but it's true: not a day goes by that I don't think about you. I miss you tremendously.

Thank you to my first boss, Mark Ehnis. You, like my wife, saw something in me—a gift. And so you gifted me my favorite book, *The War of Art* by Steven Pressfield on my twenty-fifth birthday. That book changed my life, and you did too. Thanks Mark.

Joe Kenn, the Big Doggie, thank you.

Thank you, Thomas Bowes, my former Director of Operations and my forever friend.

Molly Mahoney, my cognitive behavioral therapist in the spring of 2020, thank you for telling me: "Write your book. I can't wait to read it." Well, here it is.

Derek Hansen, one of my favorite people on the planet. Thank you for helping me become a sprinter. There are some great stories in this book because of you.

Thank you to another sprint coach of mine, Tony Holler. Your axiom, "speed grows like a tree" is not only true, but also analogous to one's gift—especially writing. Thank you for reminding me of that simple truth, as inconvenient though it may be.

Continuing the run of track coaches (pardon the pun), I have to thank Jerry Baltes, head track and field coach at my alma mater, Grand Valley State. Thank you, Jerry, for giving me the chance to compete at any and all of the NCAA meets GVSU hosts; you've never once denied me the chance to do what I love.

Thank you, Carl Valle, at *Simplifaster.* You used to tell me: "I don't want another article. I want a *Hunter* article." Well Carl, hopefully this isn't just another book. It's a *Hunter* book.

Thank you to *New York Times Bestselling Author,* Cynthia Hickey of *Winged Publications,* the woman who took a chance on me. We haven't met yet, but we will soon. Until then, you need to know this: thank you for ushering me from writer to author. Let's give this book wings and get it into as many hands as possible. Thanks Cynthia.

Thank you to my old boss during my sprint as a life insurance salesman, John. That six-month stretch we had together was fun, too much fun.

Thank you, Father Stephen Durkee for confirming the subtitle for this book—which is no small thing—do you remember what you said? "Self-sabotage to self-mastery," you said, nodding. "I like that." Thank you, Father Stephen.

What would an author be without his editor? Thank you to David T. Griffith, who has edited a number of my horror stories. So, when it came time to select an editor for my first big boy book, the choice was easy. Speaking of horror, Stephen King said, "To write is human, to edit is divine." If that's the case, Jesus had His hands on yours the entire time. Thank you, David.

Thank you, Lisa Waalkes, John Salzwedel, Pamela Keim, and the rest of the members, at the Grandville/Jenison Toastmasters Club. You three encouraged me to take part in our tiny club's Table Topics contest with the hope that I might represent us at the District Championship months from then—and I did, because of you three.

If you've ever listened to the band Avenged Sevenfold, you can tell they were heavily influenced by Metallica. Same goes for Volbeat and Godsmack. As you read this book, it won't take long before you see how much two Steves, Pressfield and King, have influenced my writing. From punchy prose like Pressfield to movie-like metaphors playing in the theater of your imagination that made King well, the king. Those two heavy hitters did a number on yours truly. To the two Steves, thank you. I could have done a lot worse than be influenced by you guys.

Steven Pressfield gets another thank you. *Hey-o!* In your book, *Do The Work,* you write about the opposite of Resistance, which is Assistance. I gotta tell you, your books, our penpal-esque friendship, and the way God used you in the hero's journey that Part Two is composed of has been nothing short of the opposite of Resistance. Thanks Steve, for being the greatest Assistance an author could ask for.

Mr. Dan S. Peña, the biggest and baddest coach and mentor I've ever had. Thank you for becoming Chairman of my Board of Directors. Thank you for the tough love. Thank you for helping me realize super success isn't for me, because when I did, I finally stopped sabotaging myself.

Thank you to my wife for helping me whittle these acknowledgments down from twenty-two pages to just over three.

And lastly, thank you Dear Reader. That'll probably be the last time I refer to you as such. My wife, after reading the manuscript, told me to ditch it. So don't get used to it. What you can get used to, however, are some kickass stories. This book is carpet bombed with those bad boys. I'm getting ahead of myself. Thank you for picking this book up. It's my hope you won't be able to put it down. And if that ends up being the case, then thank you in advance (another term my wife despises, but I think it's appropriate) for taking the time to read it. It's the greatest compliment you could ever give me.

What I Know—Part One

"We can't rewrite what's already been written, but we can start a new chapter…*today.*" — My mother, Shelly

The Way—Part One

Summer, 2005

I lived with my mom.

My dad, whom she hadn't been with since I was four years old, lived on the other side of town; but I wouldn't say he was *living* there—he was dying. A massive stroke one year prior followed by three unsuccessful surgeries in a matter of weeks to remove a tennis ball-sized brain tumor placed him in hospice.

With death being imminent, I visited him every day.

One afternoon, instead of dropping me off, my mom came inside my dad's house with me. His caretaker would be back later that night. My dad's girlfriend, Karen, and my aunt Holli were out on the stoop having a smoke. I rounded my dad's hospice bed and made for the kitchen to grab a drink out of the fridge. In my periphery, my mom placed her hand on his as he lay lifeless on a hospice bed in the living room. "Michael," she said, "do you want Hunter to be here when you go to be with Jesus?"

After the trauma of all his brain surgeries, my dad's body had resigned. He couldn't speak. He could only nod and shake his head.

Wanting to see what his answer would be, I swung a look around the corner, peering into the living room where my dad lay. I can still see the hockey-stick-shaped scar behind his ear. I can still see him, almost mechanically, shaking his head. Left and right. Left and right.

Why didn't my dad want me there when he died?

What I Know—Part Two

This book is needed, and as I once heard international marketing mogul Jay Abraham say: "That's clinical, not conceited."

How do I know this book is needed? I needed it more than anyone. I have a PhD in self-sabotage.[1] I wrote this book because I was trying to solve my own problem. I had to scratch my own itch, so to speak.

After two painful decades succumbing to the story of my life—and self-sabotage—I turned the page. I went off the script. I took my mom's advice. I started that new chapter. I changed my story. And when I changed my story, I changed my life.

This book is literal proof of that.

This is The Way: Out of Self-Sabotage; Into Self-Mastery.

January 22, 2023

"Enough of this, man." I said moments after waking. I licked my lips, then tried to swallow but couldn't. My mouth

[1] Metaphorically speaking, of course. But the idea of obtaining my PhD in this subject matter has crossed my mind.

was cotton, filled with remnants of sugar and sodium from the night before.

After opening my indoor track season[2] within one second of my all-time personal best in the 400-meter dash, I binge ate myself into oblivion hours later, wiping out weeks' worth of training leading up to the race. I set myself back to the starting line—no, behind the starting line, more like it.

Self-sabotage.

I peeled the weighted blanket off me, swung both legs off the bed, and made for my office. I rifled through my desk's drawer, fished out a marker, and wrote this question on my blackboard:

Image 1: The blackboard in my office, January 22, 2023, source: Hunter M. Charneski

That's the trillion-dollar question.

At that time, I was, as mentioned, just beginning the indoor track season. In addition to that, I was days removed from winning my local Toastmasters Table Topics[3]

[2] I'm blessed to be able to compete in NCAA track meets regularly—and am more than competitive—despite weighing at least seventy pounds more (235 pounds) and being no less than ten years older than the collegiate sprinters I race against.

[3] *Table Topics* is extemporaneous public speaking. The Contest Chair

championship, which advanced me to the Area Championship in mid-February. I was getting married in less than two weeks. I was three years into writing a horror novel—a werewolf story—and was failing miserably.

Speaking of failing, I was also in business with a gentleman internationally known as *The Trillion Dollar Man*—Dan S. Peña. Mr. Peña served as chairman of my Board of Directors for *Luminary HealthCare*, a HealthCare acquisition platform. The week of the track meet, we failed to acquire our first business. When I say we, I mean me. The deal fell apart after we signed the Letter of Intent and thank God for that.

I'll explain why later in Part Two.

Anyway, to say I was busy would be an understatement of biblical proportions. I was doing just about everything a thirty-two-year-old could do. In fact, perhaps the only thing I wasn't doing was the one thing that would have changed everything. The one thing that would answer the trillion-dollar question—writing.

Writing is my gift; from God to me and me to you.

But there was no way I was going to get anywhere near the answer to the trillion-dollar question with the kind of writing I was doing previously, which amounted to little more than mental masturbation; dipping my toe in the water instead of going all-in.

Sure, I had been published twice on *The Night's End,* an Australian podcast for horror fiction, but that came easy to me. I just made stuff up. All I had to do was throw in the necessary tropes and conventions and voila, I had a scary story.

The question also would not be answered by the kind of quasi voyeuristic writing that got me published on websites

---

presents a random question to the Speaker, who then must craft a one-to-two-and-a-half minute speech on the spot–a true test of one's speaking ability.

like *Medium* and *Simplifaster* nor in periodicals on the magazine stand at Barnes & Noble.

That dribble was more propagandistic than purposeful.

There will always be a market for articles on how to scale your startup and how to help athletes get faster and stronger—both arenas I had become an expert in, but only for dishonest gain. That kind of writing was industry exploitation instead of inner exploration.

It wasn't until I took a plunge into myself, an inner exploration, that I found *The Way*—with a capital W.

The Way couldn't be made up or monetized.

The Way involved a transformation far greater than any werewolf underwent—that's a truly scary story.

That's the kind of writing I needed to be doing; the itch I needed to scratch; the gift I needed to go all-in on; the race I needed to be running. Thank God I did. If I hadn't, I never would have been able to go off the script, to start that new chapter. I would never have been able to change my story. Thank God for that, too.

Because when I changed my story, I changed my life.

After interrogating myself on a Google Doc for several weeks; after taking what I found in my writing and refining it in speech after speech at Toastmasters; after being asked to speak to discouraged children, helping them turn life's adversities into their advantage; after being asked to speak to derelict men, helping them bridge the gap from self-sabotage to self-mastery; after doing the unthinkable, walking away from all-but guaranteed millions if not *billions* of dollars, the answer struck me.

Default.

That's why we sabotage ourselves.

What is Default?

The American Heritage® Dictionary of the English Language, 5th Edition defines default as: "Failure to perform a task or fulfill an obligation."

Francis Xavier, (1506-1522) put it more poignantly,

saying: "If you give me the child until he is seven, I will show you the man." What Xavier implied is that childhood ingrains a particular set of "obligations" in our brain's Default Mode Network (DMN) that are then observed in adulthood[4].

Consider the following examples:

When you were a kid, if you witnessed your parents being together and in love one week, then spiteful and split apart the next, is it any wonder why your relationships as a grown man are no different? The only crime your girlfriend ever committed was loving you too much.

That's a problem. That doesn't feel like love to you. So, you break her heart, then bring her back until she's beloved, then you break her heart again. It's what you witnessed mom and dad do. And that's exactly what you do.

You'd rather be alone than adored.

Maybe you were taken away from your dad when you were a toddler. Maybe he was taken from you as a teenager, dying your first week in high school. Maybe the decade between was right for all the wrong reasons. No. Maybe the decade between was right for all the *right* reasons, but by then Default had already done its thing. Maybe your mom married a guy with money, lots of money. Maybe you lacked privation i.e, you lacked *lack*; so, you played Sonic the Hedgehog on your Sega Dreamcast until noon in your underwear. Maybe that lack of privation stunted your growth, going through second adolescence in your twenties and being an overgrown infant in your thirties. Maybe being taken from your dad and then him being taken from you made you believe you're a victim and always will be. Maybe that's why you pointlessly pursue bigger and badder mentors and coaches, worshiping them to gain their approval because

[4] Damaraju et al., 2014; Gao et al., 2009; Lee, Morgan, Shroff, Sled & Taylor, 2013

you're unconsciously searching for the father you lost all those years ago. Maybe.

Did you know you had a gift in grade school? Whether it was writing, painting, singing, and the like. You weren't like everyone else, were you?

You were artistic. Your buddies on the other hand? They were athletic. In your young mind, you saw them as warriors, practically speaking.

They took first in the mile in gym class. You took last; even behind the girls.

They were three-sport athletes. You were a goalie in soccer, a glorified scarecrow, praying the ball wouldn't get by you.

Your crush, Rachel, wanted nothing to do with you and everything to do with them. Is that why you've only flirted with your gift of pottery, poetry, or photography while falling in love with the ways of the world?

What your buddies had and were doing looked like success to you. *To hell with being an artist,* perhaps you implicitly thought or felt *I want to be a warrior, too!*

All these years later, you got what you set out for. You're a warrior, alright, a fitness freak. More like a freak about your fitness—totally neurotic and rigid about every little thing until being fit looks and feels more like being sick, mentally and physically. You've got money but never have enough because you don't know what enough is, so you keep accumulating cash, corrupting your character more and more. You've got your pick with women now but are never satisfied. Sex is a drug; in the moment it's indescribably pleasurable. When it's over, you feel empty, like your soul has just been siphoned. Yeah, you got what you set out for, and you're miserable.

You're successful, but you're successfully stuck.

You know deep down you've amassed a mountain of meaningless wins. You've got everything, but you've sabotaged the one thing that could change everything—your gift; from God to you and from you to the world. Particularly, the one who needs it most. *You.*

You're starving to go all-in on your gift of theater, coaching, architecture; to be the artist you know you are. But if you did, you'd be failing to fulfill the obligations Default instilled in your childhood—so you binge eat yourself into oblivion.

Like I said, I needed this book more than anyone else—and that's absolutely clinical, definitely not conceited.

Default's obligations, or what I call, *innocent inauthenticities,* make us guilty of clinging to the catastrophes of our childhood. And here's the deal: more often than not, we do it subconsciously. Nobody wakes up thinking, *how can I sabotage myself today?* That isn't how it works. Unless you're a psychopath.

I don't think you're a psychopath, by the way. Then again, maybe you are. I don't know. In either case, it could be that you have pathologized yourself, being programmed by the tasks or obligations instilled in your childhood; you're unconscious of your unconscious thoughts. In other words, you don't think about what you think about. Your Default has a set of negative cognitions, or stories, that either implicitly or explicitly sound or feel like (and this list is by no means exhaustive):

- I am not good enough.
- I am a victim.
- I am unworthy.
- I am a loser.
- I am unfavored.

I would ask you to consider watching yourself for the next week. Better yet, in the interest of not wasting time, reflect on the past week. What did you do, or not do? Were your actions in alignment with the stories listed above?

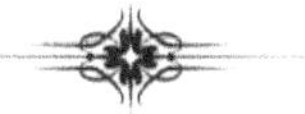

You've become so familiar with your story of feeling unworthy, not good enough, and constantly victimizing yourself, you're not even aware of it because it feels normal. Whenever you step out into the unknown, or try to scratch your own itch, be it experiencing unconditional love, a bank account not in the negative, or going all-in on your gift, Default reminds you of your story—how you're "supposed" to feel. And you self-sabotage right back to the same script you've been reading all along. The devil you know is better than the devil you don't, so the saying goes. Instead of starting that new chapter and changing your story, you go right back to page one.

Your personal reality as a child became your personality as an adult.[5]

Default.

That's why we sabotage ourselves.

Your story is keeping you stuck.

Your lens of the future is clouded by the colors of your past.

Instead of a map leading you where you want to go, all you have are memories of what you know.

But what if such a map existed? What if your future pulled you out of your past and into the present, going all-in on your gift? What if you knew a way, *The Way,* to stop self-sabotage and achieve self-mastery—to change your story?

Here is my promise to you: this book is your map; The Way to going all-in on your gift. By the end of this book, you will know how to stop self-sabotage, realizing you have the power to change your story. And when you do, get ready.

---

[5] World-renowned neuroscientist, Dr. Joe Dispenza said this while being interviewed by Ed Mylett, I thought it was brilliant.

Because when you change your story, you change your life.

Part One: Defining Default, will do exactly what the title suggests. Default will be defined in a myriad of ways. From poignant and punchy analogies and metaphors to serve as tangible examples of Default; to biblical stories that mirror anecdotal accounts in my life where I was under Default's dominion for thirty years, sabotaging myself for two-thirds of that time. Part One is going to clearly define Default, giving you peace of mind instead of Default having a piece of it.

Part Two: Redefining Default, is a documented hero's journey[6] beginning on July 7, 2022, and ending on May 11, 2023.

Before I go any further, you might be wondering: *what's a hero's journey?* I can't help but smile whenever I field that question. Reason being, you know what the hero's journey is, even if you don't realize it. It's primordial. It's the way through which you perceive the world; you see your life through the lens of a story. Which is why you unconsciously accepted that Pinocchio had to rescue his father from the abyss and be transformed in the process; why Luke Skywalker had the epic realization that Darth Vader was his decrepit father and then was spiritually reborn so he could defeat the Evil Empire; why Simba had to dispense with Hakuna Matata (being an overgrown infant) and revivify his father, Mufasa, by becoming King of Pride Rock. Each of those movies is a hero's journey. That's why we love them. Not because our lives are like movies; movies are like our lives!

Speaking of life, this is worth mentioning, Jesus Christ

---

[6] The hero's journey is a universal narrative structure through which we unconsciously perceive the world. The hero's journey was conceptualized by Joseph Campbell, who wrote, *The Hero with a Thousand Faces.*

once said: "I am the way and the truth and the life. No one comes to the Father except through me." What that means is, I think, is part and parcel with Swiss psychiatrist, Carl Jung's (1875-1961) dictum for life: *in sterquiliniis invenitur,* which in essence means: *what you most want in life will be found where you least want to look.* If you're willing to risk losing all the accouterments of success—money, material things, women, status—and go all-in on the gift you've neglected your entire life, you will finally find what success has never brought you: self-mastery.

That's the quintessential hero's journey motif.

This begs the question: what is self-mastery? Having the guts to sacrifice your self-sabotage masquerading as success—burning your Golden Calf.

Your Golden Calf is representative of the self-sabotaging activities you're sacrificing your gift for. Consider the biblical story in the book of Exodus[7]. When Moses was leading the Israelites out of Egypt—living under Pharoah's tyranny was their Default, fundamentally—he climbed Mount Sinai to receive the Ten Commandments from God the Father. While Moses was gone, the Israelites self-sabotaged, defaulting to the innocent inauthenticities of their past by casting a calf made of solid gold; worshiping a god of gold they could hold more than the God they couldn't hold; despite His gift to them, the Promised Land, being

---

[7] If you're atheist, agnostic, or secular, and are offended by the mention of the Bible or God and are now considering putting this book down because of it, I would urge you to reconsider. Doing so would be, in my estimation, an act of self-sabotage. Default would be convincing you to go back to what is most familiar to you, staying away from what you don't know. More of the same leads to more of the same. If nothing changes, nothing changes. Whether you believe in God is your business, not mine. That being said, I'm not going to maintain a belief neutrality in the coming pages, so don't let mention of Him prevent you from receiving the solution to your self-sabotage. If you give me till the end of this book, I promise you, it will be well worth your time. Deal?

worth far more than its weight in gold.

We are not so different from the Israelites. Because we feel like victims, do we not worship false gods of money, status, and success—gold we can hold—while sacrificing the gift God gave us that, if we went all-in on it, would be worth more than its weight in gold? Moral of the story? Burn the Golden Calf. It's The Way to stop self-sabotage. That's self-mastery. I should warn you, what you most want to find will be found where you least want to look. That's the hero's journey, homie.

Part Three is about knowing what to ignore. On a deeper, transformative level, Part Three will help you create a new Default for your life. On the practical side, there will be tips and tricks on how to turn your gift into gold, per se; how to turn your craft into your career. That's a good deal for any aspiring artist. On the philosophical side, there's going to be some thought-provoking stuff. From one hero's journey bleeding into the next to the lessons we learn from each manifesting themselves into our life's work. *Hey-o!* On the physical side, no longer will you have to be the warrior you aspired to be in your youth, nor do you need to feel ashamed or emasculated for embracing the artist in you. Self-mastery is about being a Master of Two Worlds, à la the hero's journey, where you can integrate both aspects of your being into a new identity others will aspire to become—an *Artistic Warrior,* perhaps? It won't be long before you begin rubbing off on other Self-Sabotaging Men. Sooner or later, they're going to seek your counsel. They'll want what you've got. And you'll help them because you'll have a new obligation to fulfill—a *moral* obligation: using your gift from God to tell your story, compelling them to change theirs.

Can you imagine if a hundred self-sabotaging men did that?

A thousand.

A *million?*

How's that for a new Default?

That is The Way.

You have a choice. You can start that new chapter today, or you can keep trying, and failing, to rewrite what's already been written.

You can scratch your own itch, or someone else's.

You can go off the script, or you can stay on the same script Default's had on your entire life, transforming only when the conditions are just right, like a werewolf, then self-sabotaging back to the overgrown infant you are after the damage has already been done.

You know the answer to the trillion-dollar question.

Default.

And now I have a question for you, one I'm not sure you can put a price on. Now that you know why you sabotage yourself, I gotta ask, haven't you had enough of that?

What I Know—Part Three

On the other side of self-sabotage lies self-mastery.

Self-mastery looks different for everyone.

Here's how it looked for me back in late October 2023.

I slept on a mattress in the basement. It wasn't glamorous, but what it lacked in pizzazz it made up for with humility and utility.

My alarm went off at seven. I slipped the eye mask off my head, let out a yawn, and sprang out of bed. My ankles popped like packing peanuts as I went up the steps.

Still half-asleep, I took a freezing cold shower. As masochistic as it sounds, I preferred it that way, and still do. If I was fully awake, I might've given it a second thought. Default loves second thoughts; second thoughts lead to self-sabotage. I never did it for the health benefits—of which I heard there are plenty—I did it because I didn't want to do it. I did it because as soon as I was out, maybe three minutes later, *then I was* fully awake and happier than a cat in a mess of guitar strings. I did it because ice water raining down on my brain and body was like liquid-dopamine. I did it because taking a cold shower drowns the stories Default might've tried to whisper in my head. I did it because that's what self-mastery looked like for me, first thing in the morning.

I got dressed and walked out to the kitchen. I made a green drink mixed with a half-teaspoon of salt and slammed it. I poured a cup of coffee for the road and knifed a pat of butter in it. *That* I did for the health benefits. My wife, Tiffany, met me by the sink, packing her lunch. I gave her a kiss, then a gentle clap on the butt. She returned the favor, on both accounts. We were still working on the proper amount of force to hitcha where the good Lord splitcha, and still are, but we're getting there. Love and laughter was, and is, self-mastery to *us,* first thing in the morning.

We were out the door by quarter after seven.

I drove her to and from work because we only had one car back then—which kinda sucked, and the fact that it had no power steering, leaking brake lines, and bald tires really sucked—but we enjoyed the quality time together.

Why didn't we fix it? We weren't broke—though we were that summer—we just couldn't swing it those days. We didn't stress about it. What good would that have done? We knew we'd be able to repair or replace it soon enough. In the meantime, we just kept on doing what we were doing—enjoying the quality time; independent of our external circumstances, independent of what others thought, and independent of what self-sabotaging activities Default desperately tried convincing us to partake in.

Said plainly, we knew what to ignore.

That's self-mastery.

By eight o'clock I was back home at my desk. I spent about half an hour reading the Bible. I put God first in my life back then, and still do now, not a Golden Calf. I knew The Way and thank God for that.

By half past it was time to write. A blank Google Doc became a canvas for creation, and the blinking cursor was its finger, as if it was curling it at me saying: "Bring it."

I accepted. I slipped my headphones on, letting Beethoven do his thing while I did mine. I wrote until my eyes hurt, which was until eleven or so. I cooked up a dozen eggs while listening to a podcast. When I finished eating, I took a ten-minute walk outside to reset before hitting the keyboard for another two-hour stretch, maybe three, I don't remember.

At two o'clock it was time to train. I'm a sprinter, both

athlete and artist, an *Artistic Warrior—hey-o!*—having integrated both aspects of my being helped me incorporate the best of both worlds.

My best writing comes when I let go, same with sprinting.

My worst writing comes when I rush, same with sprinting.

I got to the track. I warmed-up. I did a few sprints, mainly top-speed stuff that day if I recall. Or was it block-starts? To hell with it, doesn't matter. The session probably lasted less than half an hour anyways. I did what needed to be done and got on with my day.

When did I train next? When was the next race?

Couldn't tell you. Couldn't care less.

I wasn't a slave to my schedule anymore, nor was my training tyrannical—boy did it used to be, lemme tell you—I finally started running *my* race, not someone else's.

At half past three, I was parked just past the front door of the school where Tiffany teaches. I shot her a "Here" text.

She walked to the car, got in, and laid a hearty smack on my lips. I didn't complain. We chit-chatted on the way home, telling each other about our day, and continued the conversation as we transitioned from the car to our living room for thirty to forty minutes before I had to hit the bricks—my shift started fifteen minutes later.

Back then I was the Assistant Manager at a Subway restaurant just 2.9 miles down the road. I liked my job. At Subway, I did more than make sandwiches. For both my staff and customers, I tried to be a reflection of Jesus. I'm speaking for myself here: at Subway, He was The Way—and He still is, if you ask me.

I punched in just before five o'clock and asked my staff—usually one or two high school kids—if they needed anything from me. Nine times out of ten they didn't. I took a lap around the store to see what needed what. I restocked the straws, chips, and cups; did the dishes; answered the phone when it rang. Then I hopped on the line and helped my staff, making a sandwich or two—or ten—when the dinner rush hit.

A few hours later, maybe around eight, I cleaned the urinal, mopped the floor, and pulled bread for the next day.

At closing time, I let my staff take the tips. They're kids. They appreciated it. I counted the cash in the drawer, locked the door, and turned off the OPEN sign.

I did it all, man.

Image 2: Me working on this book after hours at Subway, October 14, 2023 source: Hunter M. Charneski

I remember this part vividly.

It was a little after ten. I was sitting in the manager's office—which was more like a glorified broom closet—doing my real work. I was writing this book. I was there until half past ten that night—don't worry, I clocked out at closing time. I'm no crook—I was tired, but I wanted to finish whatever chapter I was working on. Don't ask me which one, that part of the memory isn't so vivid.

When I got home the lights were off. Tiff was zonked. I didn't risk disturbing her. I walked cat-soft into my office, slipped off my work clothes, and headed downstairs.

I was zonked as soon as I shut my eyes.

The next day was no different. She was up by six at the latest, me an hour later. She got her rest, and I got mine—something both of us desperately needed until our circumstances changed. And they did, by the way.

That was October 2023. Between then and May 2024, I went from Assistant Manager to Manager; Manager to Multi-Unit Manager; then became District Manager of eight Subway restaurants in Grand Rapids, Michigan. *Hey-o!*

On the other side of self-sabotage lies self-mastery.

Self-mastery looks different for everyone.

Writing, sprinting, slingin' subs and sleeping in the basement is what self-mastery looked like for me back then, and still does. Not much has changed since—except for the sleeping in the basement part.

PART ONE: DEFINING DEFAULT

"Only a dog returns to its vomit…" – 2 Peter 2:22

SECTION I: DEFAULT AND RESISTANCE

The Victim and The Villain—Part One

Every story has a victim and a villain.

Though they're not the same, they're different sides of the same self-sabotaging coin.

The question is: which one are you?

Are you the villain? No, I don't think so. Villains don't try to better themselves. You wouldn't have picked this book up if you were the villain.

That's the good news.

The bad news is, that means you're the victim.

Fair enough.

But who, or what, is the villain?

December 6, 2015

My twenty-fifth birthday.

My boss gave me a copy of *The War of Art* by Steven Pressfield.

In it, Pressfield defines the villain; a villain he calls Resistance—with a capital R.

> *"Resistance by definition is self-sabotage,"* Pressfield

writes.

Conceptually speaking, Resistance is the voice inside your head. It pipes up the moment you sit down to write your book; to build your business plan; to paint your polyptych; to go all-in on your gift.

Resistance sounds like:

- "What're you doing? This sucks. Start over. Better yet, quit."
- "You think you've got something special to give? You're not ubiquitous or unique. Cut the crap—and the charade. You're a charlatan."
- "You're a fart-in-the-wind. Why work so hard on this when, the day after you're dead, the world will find someone else to do what you never could? And that someone will be better than you, too."

Do any of those sound germane? That's Resistance.

But this book isn't about Resistance.

This book is about Default—with a capital D.

Default has made you the victim in your own story—rather successfully, I must say, both literally and worldly.

Default, unlike Resistance, isn't the voice inside your head.

Default is deeper than that.

Default isn't heard, it's felt. Default is an implicit sense or belief that something is deeply wrong with you; wrongs that are accepted without being articulated. That acceptance leads to self-sabotage, sometimes unconsciously.

Though Default and Resistance can, and do, work in tandem to get you to self-sabotage, Resistance, like any other villain, can be defeated. The victim, or Default, on the other hand, can't be beaten. But it can be transformed, or redefined, practically speaking.

As someone who has a PhD in self-sabotage, in my

experience, transforming Default is way harder than beating Resistance. Redefining the way you see yourself is harder than engaging in self-sabotage. Which is why we stay stuck in the latter. The former is foreign and formidable.

After reading *The War of Art*, I couldn't understand why I kept sabotaging myself.

Beating Resistance wasn't super difficult. I'd hear it whisper in my head, then I'd offer a cognitive cuss in my rebuttal, and start writing. Bang. Resistance beaten.

Sooner or later, my momentum would slow down until I stopped writing completely. Those innocent inauthenticities Default planted in my childhood tricked me into looking for gold in the dirt—a new Golden Calf. A mentor or coach who helped me acquire money and notoriety, sometimes women—instead of trying to turn what I perceived as dirt, my writing, into gold.

A few months would pass.

I'd read *The War of Art* again.

I'd go on a writing sprint: sometimes a blog or two; other times a magazine would publish an article of mine. It was only a matter of time before I played the victim again, sacrificing my gift of writing for what my innocent inauthenticities thought success looked like.

This cyclical self-sabotage went on and on for almost ten years.

Why?

Because I wasn't transforming. I was beating Resistance, but ignoring Default.

I was defeating the villain at the cost of remaining the victim—and I didn't even know it.

Though Default and Resistance are not the same, they're different sides of the same self-sabotaging coin.

The Victim and The Villain—Part Two

February 22, 2024

I called my friend Glen.

Glen is a writer, too.

"Hey," I said. "I need your help."

"Sure," Glen said. "What's up?"

"I'm still having trouble clearly articulating the difference between Default and Resistance."

There was a pause, followed by a rasping sound. I imagine Glen passed a hand down his stubbled face. "Okay," Glen said. "Can you tell me the difference between Default and Resistance—in your own words?"

"Yeah," I said, then failed miserably, leaning on metaphors and analogies. They were colorful and clever. But they didn't provide the clarity he or I were hoping for. In the most literal sense, I put the cart before the horse.

After nearly an hour of Glen and I going back and forth, here's what I came up with:

- Resistance is conscious. Default is unconscious.
- Resistance is neurotic. Default is neurologic.
- Resistance uses the present. Default uses your past.

- Resistance is articulate. Default is illiterate.
- Resistance is heard. Default is felt.
- You succumb to Resistance. You act out your Default.

I'm not saying Default is the "superior" form of self-sabotage. Nor am I in any way "belittling" Pressfield's Resistance.

This isn't a Jordan or Lebron kind of debate.

This is a duality—same coin, different sides.

Resistance is conscious, able to communicate from one individual to another for mass oppression.

Default is unconscious, spreading within you for sole, and soul, possession.

Both Resistance and Default are internal. But the former grows from the soil of self-sabotaging stories while the latter is the seed.

Resistance uses words.

Default doesn't use words, so I used my own.

The Victim and The Villain—Part Three

Early Spring, 2023

I had over one hundred pages of this book written. Then I stopped, pushing my Chromebook away like it tried to gag me. Then, out of the corner of my eye, the spine of another book by Steven Pressfield, *The Artist's Journey,* stuck out from the rest of the books on the shelf. Like a hitchhiker thumbing for a ride, it was waiting for me to pick it up. And trust me, like what Hollywood calls a *Deus Ex Machina* (God in the Machine, i.e., divine intervention), it wasn't just waiting, it was *wanting* me to pick it up.

On the first page, Pressfield writes:

At least once a day
(sometimes three or four),
someone sends me an e-mail
describing, with excruciating
vividness, their losing
struggle with their own
Resistance. Many of these
letters are heartbreaking.
They plead for help. 'How'
they ask, 'can I stop
drinking/doing drugs/self-
destructing/beating my
spouse/neglecting my

> *children and start doing my best work/my soul's desire? How can I keep up my will to fight?*
>
> *In Hollywood terms, we would say of these writers that they are at their All Is Lost moment.*
>
> *They are at that point in their hero's journey where they are as far from their objective as possible.*
>
> *They are torn between their daimon—the inheriting spirit summoning them to live out their highest destiny—and the very real demands and fears of the material world in which they (and their families) dwell.*

Unlike those who emailed Pressfield, I wasn't at my All Is Lost moment, but I was close.

However, like them, I was torn between my daimon (my gift of writing) and the very real demands of the material world.

After then, I knew those who emailed Pressfield weren't losing to Resistance. They were losing to their Default—they were victims in their own stories and they didn't even know it.

I knew I wasn't the only one who needed this book.

I knew those who emailed Pressfield needed it.

I knew *you* needed it, too.

Your best work is still ahead of you. Your soul's desire is God's desire for you, that's why He gave you the gift you're willing to fight for. And by virtue of the fact that you're reading this book, I know you've got a little fight left in you.

If that's the case, then All Is Not Lost.

Not for you.

SECTION II: DEFAULT AND SELF-SABOTAGE

Default and the Daimon—Part One

Default is a demon, the devil you know.

A *demon* is the antithesis of an angel. Demons have intractable obsessions with harmful deeds—deeds like self-sabotage.

The *daimon* is akin to the muse, a being somewhere between God and human. The daimon is your own personal angel, ministering to you to go all in on your gift. Whether it's writing, singing, painting, whatever. It's a gift—to you and from you to the world.

Default and your daimon are waging war inside you as we speak. The side of who you are versus the side of who you could become.

Who wins?

The one you side with.

Whose side are you on?

Default and the Daimon—Part Two

The Ancient Greeks thought of the daimon as *the ghost of a fallen hero.*

Your daimon is the ghost dwelling inside you, your fallen hero, your gift.

The viscerally ill feeling you get when you fall victim to Default is the daimon wrestling inside of you, scratching and clawing to get out.

The daimon is begging you to let it out of the cage you've put it in.

It's calling out to you from *inside* you.

It wants you to revive your fallen hero.

Many will never know this. Some do, but knowledge isn't enough. Only a few are brave enough to exorcize and do battle with their own demons to unleash, or resurrect, the daimon.

Why?

Default.

Default deploys many demons, but there is only one daimon.

Are you brave enough to do battle with Default and its horde of demons?

Are you willing to let parts of you die—almost all of you, in fact—for the daimon; to revive the fallen hero inside you; to be spiritually reborn?

Default and Handsaws

Default is like a tree in our backyard—the one missing some branches.

Every time you go out on a limb to write that novel, start that business, paint that portrait, you test your mettle—Default meddles with your mind. And so, you take a handsaw to the branch you're sitting on.

Self-sabotage.

On and on this goes until the tree in your backyard doesn't have any branches left.

You repeat what you don't repair.

That's Default.

Default and Wanderers

J.R.R. Tolkien once said: "Not all who wander are lost."

I agree with him.

Not *all* who wander are lost. But the majority of Self-Sabotaging Men who wander are precisely that—lost.

According to Google, which uses *Oxford Languages, wander* is defined as: "to walk or move in a leisurely, casual, or aimless way."

To be aimless means you're without an aim. And if you're without an aim, then you don't know where you're going; you don't know where you are.

That's a problem.

But don't take it from me, take it from someone way smarter than me. Dr. Jordan B. Peterson said: "If you don't know where you're going, then you don't know what you're doing."

In other words, *most* who wander *are* lost.

Default loves it when you're lost because you don't know what you're doing; which is tough because most Self-Sabotaging Men have no clue where or what they're doing or where they're going.

The writer's words wander on the blank page.

The pianist's fingers wander on the keys.

The sprinter's mind wanders on the track.

Default knows it's only a matter of time before you start sabotaging yourself back to the people, places, and things you *do know.* You self-sabotage until you know where you are; until you know what you're doing.

Being stuck in a self-sabotage mode masquerading as success is easier, less frightening than wandering; than going all-in on your gift of writing, singing, or painting; than finding your way in the world—finding The Way.

Not all who wander are lost, but most are.

Default devours those who wander.

Default and the Disease of More—Part One

Speaking of wandering, those who do may not be lost. But they may fall ill; ill with something I call the *Disease of More.* A short story in the Bible called *Quail from the Lord* illustrates this concept poignantly.

Here's what happened, roughly speaking:

As Moses led God's Chosen People—a multitude of six hundred thousand Israelites—out of Egypt and toward the Promised Land, a small faction of elders approached Moses one day.

"Y'know," they said. "We've been wandering in the damn wilderness for a while now, and we're thankful for the free manna your God continues to provide and all—"

"There's a *but* coming, I presume?" Moses said.

The Israelites swung looks at each other, then one said: "Would it kill Him to give us some delicious meat? I mean, don't get us wrong. Egypt was a hellhole. And Pharaoh was a real peach. But we had a smorgasbord—all at no cost! The fish and cucumbers and melons sure made the tyranny easier to swallow."

That's Default.

There's their self-sabotaging behavior.

The Israelites believed they were, and I'm quoting God here: "better off in Egypt" despite the fact that He was leading them to something better than they could have ever imagined—the gift of freedom; a land of milk and honey. God, through Moses, was showing them The Way out of self-sabotage and toward self-mastery.

The Israelites, like today's Self-Sabotaging Men, preferred to be the victim in their own story because they couldn't have a binge of biblical proportions; because they wanted what looked, felt, and tasted like success.

And they wanted more of it.

You can imagine how well their lack of gratitude sat with God. They wanted meat. He gave them meat, all right. A large wind drove in quail to their camp, as far as a day's walk in any direction.

For the next thirty-six hours or so, the Israelites went out and collected quail.

While they ate—with the meat still between their teeth—God struck them with a severe plague because of their lack of gratitude for the provisions on their way to the Promised Land.

A lack of gratitude is a symptom of Default; of being a victim.

It doesn't matter if you're wandering.

It doesn't matter if you're not lost.

It doesn't matter if you're eating manna from the hand of God.

Why doesn't it matter?

Because for the Self-Sabotaging Man, it's never enough. Their lack of gratitude and victimhood makes them fall ill with the Disease of More.

More money.

More women.

More notoriety.

More success.

Default loves it when you want more, because you could be just one more *want* away from self-sabotage.

Default Is Environmental

I spent the first eight years of my career in the strength and conditioning industry.

One of the first things I learned was the S.A.I.D. principle.

S.A.I.D. stands for *Specific Adaptations for Imposed Demands.*

What it means is, whatever the athlete is exposed to, i.e., his environment is what he will become. For example, if he is exposed to a sprint-centric training program, then he's going to become faster. If he's exposed to the weightroom, then he's going to become stronger. If he's exposed to metabolic conditioning, then he's going to become more fit.

If you want to become a bestselling author, a renowned pianist, an opera singer, then your environment needs to impose those demands in order to achieve the "specific adaptation."

A bestselling author needs unadulterated time in a quiet room to write.

A renowned pianist needs access to a working piano in a studio so he can hear each keystroke the way his audience desires to.

An opera singer needs a theater for the acoustics and atmosphere so he can really flex his pipes.

Unfortunately, most Self-Sabotaging Men's environments impose a different demand in order to fulfill the obligation, or their specific adaptation, of their Default.

Their obligations and frivolities take precedence over their gift.

Default's environment is hard to break out of once you've adapted to it—just ask the Israelites.

Default is environmental.

Default Is Mental, Too

Thomas à Kempis once said: "Wherever you go, there you are."

If you're surrounded by self-sabotage (booze, wanton relationships with women, malevolent mentors), then get the hell out of there. Unfortunately, more often than not, changing your environment isn't enough. I ought to know, I have a PhD in self-sabotage, remember?

Default is just as much mental as it is environmental, if not more so.

Again, take the Israelites for example. They left their environment, but Default didn't leave them.

Wherever they went, there they were.

Default is mental, too.

Default and Better Parents

During my time in the strength and conditioning industry, I must have attended at least a hundred seminars, clinics, and workshops.[8] At each and every one, *speed* was discussed ad nauseam. And no wonder. Speed is the one thing every athlete wants, regardless of sport.

Can speed be trained and developed?

Yes. See the S.A.I.D. principle.

Do genetics trump training?

I'd say so, and as I heard one presenter say: "You should have picked better parents."

You could say the same about Default.

If your parents moped around in the muck and the mire—and did so during your childhood—is it a surprise that your Default is that of a victim, of being unfavored, or unworthy? With stories like those playing in your subconscious, it's no wonder why you never finish your narrative nonfiction series, record your album, or discover a cure for cancer.

Are you thinking of the same question I am?

Can you "train" yourself to stop self-sabotage?

---

[8] Looking back, I can't help but laugh. Strength and conditioning coaches are really just self-help junkies with bigger arms and lower resting heart rates.

Yes. Again, see the S.A.I.D. principle.

I ask again: do genetics trump training?

Sure do. But that doesn't mean you can't change. And that doesn't mean the change will be fast, either. Take me for example. With no genetic predisposition for speed, it took me six years of diligent training to run twenty-two miles per hour. To put that in perspective, I ran a 4.9-second forty-yard dash at twenty-six years old, and a 4.44-second forty-yard dash at thirty-two.

With no familial predisposition to self-mastery, it took me over three times as long to "train" myself out of self-sabotage. Case in point: if I wanted to be a speed demon and immune to self-sabotage, I should have picked better parents.

But I didn't have any control over who my parents were.

Neither did you. You got the hand you were dealt.

That leaves you with two options:

1. You can stay in the same story of self-sabotage.

- or -

2. You can start "training" your way out of it. You can start by changing your environment; apply the S.A.I.D. principle. Do that for a few months, maybe even a few years, and you'll begin to change your story—maybe even your genetics—so you can publish that book, write your screenplay, or start that nonprofit.

I don't know about you, but the second option sounds like a better way—The Way.

Default and Life's Burn Pile

Speaking of hands being dealt, I played a lot of poker in middle school—Texas Hold 'Em more often than not.

For those who haven't played, here's the skinny.

Each player is dealt two cards.

After a round of betting, the dealer places three cards face down, which is called "burning" and then places three cards face up. Another round of betting ensues, followed by the dealer burning one card, then turning another face up. The process repeats one final time—a round of betting followed by another "burn and turn" if you will, leaving five cards face up on the board for the players.

The players' jobs are to make the best five-card hand they can by using the two cards they were dealt in concordance with the five cards the dealer dealt face up.

Pretty simple, right?

I played a lot with a buddy of mine. After every hand, this dude would, without fail, turn over the face down cards (the "burn pile") and look to see if the card(s) he needed to win the hand were in there—even though the burn pile was completely useless. It was an exercise in futility.

I thought it was bizarre.

"Why are you doing that?" I'd ask him. "The burn pile doesn't matter. You're just looking for disappointment."

He never had an answer, probably because he was under the dominion of Default.

Default is mental.

Is there a “burn pile” in your life?

Do you rummage through things that don’t matter instead of focusing on what does—like your gift? Do you go looking for disappointment in your past rather than playing the hand life dealt you the best you can?

Why are you doing that?

If you’re doing that, stop.

Default Is Cyclical

This is how you stay successfully stuck in self-sabotage:

1. You've got it all. Money, women, notoriety, and the approval of the latest and greatest mentor in your life. You've spent a great deal of time, money, and energy sabotaging yourself with a veneer of success because it feels good, but there's also a sunk cost bias attached to your success—you've invested too much in these innocent inauthenticities to turn your back on them now, right? You've got everything—but you're neglecting the one thing that would change everything. *In sterquiliniis invenitur.*

2. After a while, your soul starts to feel in error, so to speak. You're successful, but you're successfully stuck; sacrificing your gift for another accoutrement, achievement, or accolade. You get an office with a view. You earn Executive Council status as a life insurance salesman. You start a business in the same industry as your former boss because he didn't give you the sixty-three percent raise you thought you deserved.

3. Something happens—a *Deus Ex Machina*, the Hollywood term for "God in the machine," remember? An opportunity presents itself for you to use your gift, even if it's only a moment. A blog to raise money for a friend in need. A song to sing at a wedding. A consultation for a struggling business.

> And here's the thing: you kill it. The blog you wrote generates tens of thousands of dollars. The song you sang leaves not a dry eye in the church. Your vision saves a business from bankruptcy. You have no clue why. You just wrote, sang, or said whatever came to you.

In a fleeting moment of self-realization, you think *now this is what I'm supposed to be doing.* You're euphoric. You unveil the new *You* all over social media; proclaiming you're now a writer, a singer, an entrepreneur, and the like.

In other words, you go all-in on your gift. But here's the rub: nobody cares. More than that, they're repelled. You're a leper to your audience now.

Look at it from their perspective. For as long as it's taken to gain their trust that you're the authority on a certain subject matter, to go off the script and say you're now a poet, a violinist, or motivational speaker? That would be like being halfway through *Harry Potter and the Sorcerer's Stone,* then turning the page and finding yourself reading *The Shining.*

Your audience is going to be completely lost, pissed off in some cases, because they'll feel as though you've led them astray. They'll feel lied to—because they have been.

Sure, you might have changed your story—whoopie-doo for you, chief—but that's not the story your audience signed up for in the first place. They didn't subscribe to your YouTube channel so you could completely change the narrative and your offering six months later. Dudes don't follow Andrew Tate so they learn how to bake chocolate pies, they want to learn how to make money.

The moment you scratch your own itch is the moment you lose momentum with the masses.

Your business suffers.

Your Instagram following tanks.

You're alone in the wilderness.

Then Default happens.

1. You've wandered from what you know. Where you're at feels foreign, fictional even.

2. You get resentful and bitter toward your audience thinking: *this is who I really am! Don't they get it? I've got something good here! For Chrissake, if they'd just stick around long enough they'd find out they'd be blown away by my writing, my startup, my coaching!*

3. Spoiler alert: they don't stick around long enough to find out. And to be upset they don't is the wrong way of looking at it. That's a victim's perspective. The way you should look at it is through the same lens as you did before, knowing it would take time to gain your audience's trust, or—and perhaps this would be the preferred path—regaining the trust of those you lost, so they can be encouraged and empowered to change their stories too. But that's not what you do. Like I was for far too long, you're an overgrown infant and you want success right effing now. So, you go back to what you know. Only this time, you catch the Disease of More so you can ensure that next time you go all-in on your gift, you have enough money stowed away that will afford you the time to do so. You hire an even bigger and badder mentor (another Golden Calf) to make damn sure it happens, taking his every word as if it's the Word of God. Sooner or later you've got it all. Women. Money. Notoriety. And the approval of the mentor you've come to idolize.

Round and round it goes—perhaps for twenty-years.
That's how you stay stuck in self-sabotage.
Default is cyclical.

Default and Shadow Careers

Here's the thing about victims, they've got two jobs.

- Make the hero look good.
- Make the villain look bad.

That sucks for you, my guy, and here's why: it keeps you in the dark, or what Steven Pressfield calls a *shadow career.*

Pressfield writes in his book, *Turning Pro:*

> *Sometimes, when we're terrified of embracing our true calling, we'll pursue a shadow calling instead. The shadow career is a metaphor for our real career. Its shape is similar, its contours feel tantalizingly the same. But a shadow career entails no real risk. If we fail at a shadow career, the consequences are meaningless to us.*

Are you writing blogs for websites when you know you've got a book in you?

Are you writing horror instead of self-help because you're too scared to help yourself?

Are you copywriting for a women's jewelry company because it's easier to sell gold you can hold than the gold your future holds—by writing what you're supposed to?[9]

I'm asking for a friend, of course, I told you I needed this book more than anyone.

When you engage in the pointless pursuit of a shadow career, you're making the hero (your gift) look good and the villain look bad.

You're a victim, and now that you're aware of it, it's your choice whether you're going to stay in the darkness of a shadow career.

---

[9] I can only speak for writing, but I assume there is a shadow career for every Self-Sabotaging Man, regardless of what his gift is.

Default and Antibiotics

My older brother—he and I had different dads, that's why he wasn't mentioned earlier—was one of those kids who would, when sick, take his antibiotics religiously; until he felt better.

A few days would go by and wouldn't you know it? He was sick again.

So, he'd start retaking his prescription until the bottle was empty.

A few more days went by. He'd get sick again.

That stirred my mom up worse than a fart in a fan factory.

She'd have to get him a new prescription—stronger than the first—then my older brother would have to take the antibiotics all over again.

You're so familiar with feeling like a victim, unworthy, and not good enough. Once you stop feeling and believing those negative stories—which is bound to happen when you go all-in on your gift, even briefly—you return to self-sabotage just so you can affirm those same stories you've been justifying your life with for as long as you can remember—no different than how my brother would cut his medication short because of a false sense of feeling well.

That's how Default works.

You can't help it.

It's what you know.

Feeling *better* feels borrowed.

You don't own it.

You feel obligated to give it back because you've failed to fulfill the obligations and innocent inauthenticities Default instilled in your childhood.

I hate to break it to you, but there isn't a vaccine, antibiotic, or antidote for Default, so you might as well take a shot at it with an anecdote. Change your story. Change your life.

Default and Lifelong Caterpillars

I'm not a big meme guy.

But I do like the one where a butterfly and caterpillar are seated at a table conversing.

"You've changed," said the caterpillar.

The butterfly tilts its head. "We're supposed to," it said.

Don't be surprised when your friends or family or coworkers aren't cheering you on for changing, for starting that new chapter as you tackle that werewolf story you've been dying to write, launch that telecommunications company you know the market so desperately needs, take a sabbatical to train for the Olympics because you know that gold medal in the 400-meter dash is yours to lose.

Misery, in fact, does love company.

They won't like the fact that you've put down your victimhood and picked up some accountability, and agency, for your life.

People don't like putting down their victimhood. Because when they do, they can't blame others for their problems.

They have to change.

Change is hard, which is why most don't, even though we're supposed to.

Default Is a Judge

A firefighter came into Subway one day.

"I'll have the All-American Club," he said, then raised a finger. "But instead of American cheese, let's do pepperjack."

"Fair enough," I said. "Regular, or double?"

He pursed his lips, shaking his head. "Regular is fine. Double [cheese] isn't necessary."

"Well," I said, shrugging. "You might need it. I mean, you *do* run into burning buildings."

We shared a laugh.

Then he frowned. "Y'know," he said. "I'm scared to death to get up and speak to a bunch of people. But I have no problem charging into a fire."

I nodded, then said, "fire doesn't judge you."

"Puh," the firefighter said. "You got that right."

But Default does judge you, doesn't it?

Default judges you harshly. So harshly, you'd probably run into a burning building rather than make the first keystroke on a blank Google Doc; write the first lyric of your hit single-to-be; or present a business plan to a group of potential investors.

Therein lies the paradox. In the long run, letting Default convince you to self-sabotage is infinitely more dangerous than finding The Way out of self-sabotage.

I'm not saying The Way will be easy.

It’ll be hard.
It’ll be long.
Double cheese will be necessary.

Default Doesn't Care

In 2011, a YouTube video titled "Honey Badger Doesn't Care" was all the rage.

Default, like the Honey Badger, doesn't care.

- It's fearless.
- When it's hungry, it eats.
- It can run backwards, like Default runs backwards to your early years.
- It takes whatever it wants.
- It digs deep into your desires—and dreads.
- It has no regard for anyone, or anything.
- It chases.
- It will charge into a hornets' nest enduring thousands of stings, just so it can take what it wants.

What does Default want?

It wants your gift, and it doesn't care what it takes to get it. Because if it doesn't get your gift, then you won't know Default anymore. And if you don't know Default, then, like the Honey Badger, you'll no longer care.

Default's Gateway Drug

Stay off social media.

I know that's an absolutist statement, but for me—and most Self-Sabotaging Men, I presume—it's an absolute must.

Social media is a Gateway Drug for Default.

Let me be clear: I'm not saying *get off* social media, I'm saying *stay off.* The distinction needs to be made because so many businesses, perhaps yours included, use social media for lead generation and/or as a profit center.

If that's the case for you, *getting off* social media would be self-sabotage.

Staying off social media looks more like delegating it to a staff member or spouse. If you're single and a one-man show, then schedule your posts, do what you need to do, and get outta dodge. Put all social media apps in a folder on your phone labeled "Default" if you have to.

That's what I do.

It works for me.

Don't kid yourself. No matter how mentally tough you think you are, the algorithm will sell you on sabotaging yourself. Social media is fertile ground for self-sabotage—it's mental to the nth degree, so is Default.

- The Screen Queens on your explore page will make you question the perfectly good relationship you're currently in. You'll start thinking about dumping your girlfriend just so you can slide into some beautiful blonde's DMs whose AI filters make her look too amazing to be real—she isn't real, by the way. But once you start thinking about it, the more likely the thought turns into action. And if it doesn't turn into action, you'll start acting out toward your girlfriend. One day her unconditional love will feel like poison. You push her away, slowly but surely. In a paradoxical complexity, your victimhood will keep *you* from doing the deed, breaking up with her, so you continue to act like an overgrown infant—raging, pouting, being cold and crass—until one day your girlfriend says to hell with this and leaves you. Then you can have all the imaginary relationships you want with @bigbootygirl69 until you realize it's a fake account, or she's just fake in general. Talk about a Golden Calf, man.

- Those who've done what you're too afraid of—going all-in on a similar gift you have—makes you ultra-resentful of them. Not only have they written their book, composed their symphony, painted their collection, but they've done so in a remarkably meaningful way. They've taken all their life's adversities and turned it to their advantage. They've used their gift to find The Way out of self-sabotage—something you're too afraid to do. So, you don't, ever.
- The twenty-one year-old gajillionaire whose IQ is below 100 but has everything—he's what C.S. Lewis would call a *Materialistic Magician*—makes you punt a career that's doing nothing but providing for your family. Why? To do whatever that kid is doing, obviously, because you've got the Disease of More.

You don't have to get off social media. But if you're, and I mean this derogatorily, *getting off* on social media, then *stay off* social media.

Social media is a Gateway Drug for Default.

Default and Going All-In

Going all-in on your gift is a dichotomy.

Yes, you need to go all-in on your gift—but not at the expense of your expenses. Kinda like the time I abdicated all my responsibilities so I could dedicate one hundred percent of my time to writing a novel, only to wake up one morning with forty-four bucks in my checking account. That tends to happen when you're a thirty-year-old teenager writing for weeks on end while carelessly blowing your funds on create-your-own salads from MOD Pizza. Meanwhile, the autopay on my car and mortgage were still being taken out of my checking account—and I wasn't checking it.

Yes, you need to go all-in on your gift, just as long as you're not sabotaging yourself in the process.

Default and Problems—Part One

How many times have you made a problem worse than it was?

More than that, how many times have you *knowingly* made a problem worse than it was? What's more, how many times have you made a problem worse than it was just to affirm, in some sick and twisted way, that you were "right" all along? Subconsciously, you wanted to prove yourself right about being a victim, unfavored, or unworthy.

There have been so many times, during a sprint workout, I've felt a twinge or a bulge in my leg after a run.

I think I might have just pulled something, I'd think on my walk back. I would get discouraged, just like anyone else. No one likes getting hurt. But then, after catching my breath, I'd walk back to the starting line—ready to sprint again.

I was telling myself: *I better do one more just to make sure.*

POW!

Sure enough. I'd take off, and by ten meters there'd be a searing-hot pain in the hamstring, or lower leg.

If I didn't pull something on the previous rep, I sure did on the next.

I made my problem worse—a lot worse—just to prove

myself right.

How many times have you made it ninety-nine percent of the way through your novel or album only to find one chapter or song not on theme? Instead of tending to the wound, either by weaving the theme in or performing surgery, you cast it aside to rot in the land of Derelict Google Docs just to prove yourself right.

There! You think to yourself. *See? I suck! I knew it!*

Default and Problems—Part Two

I'm not convinced problems are inherently bad, quite the contrary. In fact, Without problems, there's no story. I'll take it a step further. The bigger the problem, the better the story.

Think about it. Any great movie you've seen does two things:

- Introduces a problem in the opening scene.
- Makes the problem really, really big.

For instance, if you go up to a total stranger, I'm willing to bet they know who Thanos is. But if you ask that same person who Steppenwolf is, they're probably going to tell you they don't speak German.

Case in point. Marvel did what D.C. failed to do.

- Marvel introduced Thanos in the opening scene of *Avengers: Infinity War.*
- *Justice League* introduced Steppenwolf twenty-minutes in. By then it was too late.
- Marvel made Thanos (the problem) really, really big. In fact, they made Thanos the main character.
- Steppenwolf was just another bad guy, nothing more.

- *Avengers: Infinity War* was the highest grossing movie of all-time.
- *Justice League* had to be remade.

Your story has a big problem. Its name is Default. The bigger the problem, the better the story. Use your gift to tell that story, won't you?

Default and Story—Part One

This chapter was originally titled, "Default's Slogans" because of the etymology of the word *slogan.* Slogan is derived from two Welsh words: *sluagh* and *gairm,* which literally mean *battle cries of the dead.*

But you're not dead. You're a victim. Your story isn't over yet. You can start that new chapter. But first, you've got to know your story before you can change it. This list, though not nearly complete, might resonate with some of the stories you're unconsciously feeling; unconsciously living out in self-sabotage.

- I am not good enough.
- I am less than.
- I am a loser.
- I am a victim.
- I deserve to be a victim.
- I am unlucky.
- I am unlovable.
- I am miserable.
- I deserve my misery.
- I am unworthy.
- I am alone.
- I deserve my loneliness.
- I am hopeless.
- I am helpless.
- I am useless.

- I deserve to be hopeless and helpless and useless.
- I am afraid.
- I am the worst.
- I am lost.
- I am better off dead.
- I'm retarded.[10]
- I deserve to be dead.
- I am not a writer, painter, singer, athlete, or entrepreneur.
- I don't deserve to be a writer, painter, singer, athlete, or entrepreneur.
- I am stupid.
- I am effed up.
- I am effed up beyond any and all repair.
- I am stupid and effed up for even thinking I am, or could be, a writer, painter, singer, athlete, or entrepreneur.
- I am doomed.
- I am a failure.
- I deserve to fail.
- I deserve to work a nine-to-five, get a gold watch when I retire, get on Medicare, then die.
- I suck.

These stories, and many like them, are keeping you stuck in self-sabotage. These stories are your Default. If you don't change them, and soon, they just might become your slogans—*battle cries of the dead.*

---

[10] It isn't my intention to be derogatory or insensitive. It's only my intention to be as real and relevant as possible. If I've felt–and believed I was–retarded, chances are you might have as well. To not acknowledge that reality would be truly insensitive.

Default Is a Hydra

The Hydra is an immortal, many-headed serpentine dragon that haunted the swamps around Lake Lerna in Ancient Greece. The Hydra is an amalgam of Default; each head being another story from a previous chapter; each a malevolent representation of your past experiences feeding on the present and hoarding the gold your future holds—the gold on the other side of going all-in on your gift.

Default is a Hydra. Slay one dragonhead and another will take its place.

One head might be: *I am a victim,* manifesting in your life as idolatry.

Another may be, *I am not good enough,* leading to achieving more vaporous victories.

Dispensing with all the dragons of your past won't be easy, nor quick. Trust me, it took me twenty years to slay the first. But like most things in life, the first time is always the most difficult.

To put it into perspective, slaying my second Default took four-months—*sixty-times* faster than the first (assuming the arithmetic is accurate).

My third Default? *Forty-two days.*

Once you recognize your Defaults, you won't keep your sword sheathed. You'll be less hesitant to bloody your blade. But be warned, when you slay your Default's dragons, you'll be killing a piece of yourself in the process; carving away flesh that's decaying; slicing sepulchers off your soul.

Don't be discouraged.

Yes, it will be painful. Your past always is.

Yes, you might suffer in direct proportion to the size of the Hydra's head. But the suffering will not only be temporary, it will be rewarding. When you kill the entire dragon, you get the gold your future holds.

Default and Outliers

I once heard radio talk show host and writer, Dennis Prager say: "The outlier saves every civilization."

Default makes us the exact antithesis of the outlier; we're Lifelong Caterpillars; we never finish our antibiotics; we should have picked better parents; we always want more of everything while sacrificing the one thing that would change everything.

Are you an outlier?

Are you willing to be?

Default, Idols, and God

As a victim for more than twenty years, I lived a life of idolatry—worshiping Golden Calves in the forms of coaches, mentors, and business partners. I took everything they said as the Word of God.

I'm not alone on this.

Which begs the question: why? Why do so many Self-Sabotaging Men study these figures religiously? Sure, they may be able to wipe their butt with one-hundred-dollar bills for the rest of their lives, but just like you and me, they still partake in the particularly unsavory act.

Here's why I think so. Below is a list of influential figures in the personal development and wealth creation space. To say they are appealing to today's Self-Sabotaging Man would be about as useful as pissing into a hurricane. To today's Self-Sabotaging Men, these guys are Titans of Testosterone. Financial Figureheads. Golden Calves.

- Renowned performance coach Ed Mylett is tangible. God is intangible—no physical form.
- Business magnate Andy Frisella is morally similar to you and I—having human desires of personal excellence. God is morally dissimilar to you and I—having divine desires of expanding His kingdom instead of building yours.
- *The Trillion Dollar Man,* Dan S. Peña is comprehensible. God is incomprehensible.

- Today's Self-Sabotaging Men can twist these men's teachings into their own self-sabotaging stories. Good luck trying to twist God.
- Worshiping these men often leads to materialism, even if that isn't their intention. Worshiping God involves sacrifice.
- Worshiping modern day Hugh Hefner, Dan Bilzerian involves sexual immorality. Worshiping God involves purity and commitment.
- Worshiping the internet influencing Paul brothers, Jake and Logan, may lead to doing whatever you want regardless of the consequences. Worshiping God involves doing what is best for you with accountability.
- Worshiping these men may lead to focusing on yourself. Worshiping God involves focusing on others.

In short, today's Self-Sabotaging Men follow these men because they're victims; they see these men as their savior.

Big mistake.

I'm not saying these men don't have value if they're pursued, or followed, for the right reasons. Nor is it my intention to slam any of these individuals. It's only my intention to call it how I see it so you can see it—either as I do or in your own meaningful, thought-provoking way.

The mistake most Self-Sabotaging Men make is when they put these individuals above God. They sacrifice the gift God gave them for the fleeting chance to wipe their butts with one- hundred-dollar bills for the rest of their lives.

If God gave you the gift of poetry, music, or culinary art, is it a quantum leap to assume He'd provide you with toilet paper if things got to that point?

These men are successful, yes. Are they successful because they've stuck to the gift God gave them, and after years and years of patience, He rewarded them? Or are they, like you and I, successfully stuck—accruing more and more meaningless wins as a result of their own Default of victimhood—just at a much larger scale?

It's worth thinking about.

In either case, it's evident to me that, even if you don't consider yourself a Christian, you could do a lot worse than follow Christ's teachings instead of internet influencers and the like—your Golden Calves. Because when you worship, or believe in, something other than a mere man, you gain the power to change your story instead of mimicking theirs.

And when you change your story, you change your life.

This is The Way.

A New Default—Part One

"The supreme art of war is to subdue the enemy without even fighting." – Sun Tzu

That's Default's strategy against you—and it's been undefeated.

But you're different now.

You know the enemy.

You're not like everyone else anymore.

You're an outlier.

If Default wants to continue to subdue you with self-sabotage, then it will need to fight—something it's never done before.

Advantage: you.

But having the advantage doesn't guarantee victory.

Your opponent isn't external.

It's internal.

It's you against you.

It's your Default versus your daimon; gold you can hold versus your gift from God.

It's the devil you know versus the fallen hero you've forsaken.

It's the failure to rewrite what's already been written versus starting that new chapter... *today.*

SECTION III: MY DEFAULT

Default, Families, and Lies

Families are fifty percent lies.

Read that again, four of the eight letters that make up the word are l-i-e-s.

And to prove it to you, here's a bit of my backstory.

I was three years old when my parents broke up—the first time.

Broke up isn't the truth. They *fractured*—in several places.

And no wonder, my dad had a tennis ball-sized tumor in his brain and was none the wiser to it. He couldn't remember things he said or did. He had a helluva time with simple math. He struggled with remaining committed. He was an elevator, suffice to say. Up and down he went depending on which button my mom pushed. It wasn't her fault, and it wasn't his. Neither knew of the rare form of glioma cancer housed in my dad's head. And so they'd be together one week, separated the next, and I was caught in the crossfire. This merry-go-round-like relationship painted a strange picture for me as to what love looked like—it painted a lie. Round and round it went for more than a year.

When my dad started seeing double, he went to the doctor. My dad called my mom to tell her the news. He was bawling so hard, she didn't know it was him at first. He told her he had a brain tumor. It was invading supportive tissues of his brain, eating my dad's thoughts, making him act out.

These were the doctor's words, not mine. And my dad's struggles contributed to the end of his and my mom's relationship.

They split for good when I was four. My mom had me start seeing a psychiatrist—Chuck was his name, God love 'em—shortly after; a smart move on her part. Chuck was a Guardian Angel. Had it not been for my mom's foresight and Chuck's playful, Piagetian approach,[11] God only knows how I would have turned out.

It wasn't long before my mom met another man, Andy.

Andy's a good man. Andy provided in ways my dad could not.

They went on their first date in April of 1995, were engaged at the end of July, and got married in late September.

After the wedding, Andy legally adopted me. A new dad and a new last name[12] was a lot for a four-year old. I remember the weirdness of referring to someone who wasn't my dad as exactly that. It was like someone poured molasses over my interior gears. It didn't compute. My little, forty-eight-month-old brain knew it was a lie. Oh and, little did I know, I wouldn't see my biological dad again until I was thirteen.

Before my seventh birthday, my mom and Andy had a son—my little brother, Jacob. Andy favored Jacob. I don't blame him. Jacob was his own flesh and blood. But I will say this, the favoritism toward Jacob over time led to my new Default of feeling unfavored, that's for sure. Especially when the favoritism led to a few regrettable moments of Andy not being *Father of the Year,* shall we say?

---

[11] Jean Piaget's axiom was that children need to play, explore, and experiment to gain information to better understand their world.

[12] My last name was Hilliard from the ages four to sixteen before I changed it back to Charneski.

To this day, Andy and I remember those moments very differently. Because of those moments, Andy and I were estranged for almost twenty years—beginning not long before my biological dad died.

Does it really matter what happened in those moments—or who's "right"?

I don't think so. That's not the point. I love my mom. I love Andy. If they weren't part of my backstory, then I wouldn't have much of a story to share.

The point is, families are fifty percent lies, and my backstory served as the introduction to the story of my life.

Round and round that story went for more than twenty years.

Default and "No"

I didn't take well to being told "no" when I was under the age of five.

Whenever I heard that word, I made a beeline for the closet and stayed there for what felt like hours.

It's a miracle I never crapped my pants.[13]

Is today's Self-Sabotaging Man any different? Does he like rejection; being told "no"?

A Self-Sabotaging Man hates that word. It makes him hyper self-conscious.

It's humiliating.

"No" hurts.

But it gets worse.

"No" is a double-edged sword for Default for the Self-Sabotaging Man.

"No" can either paralyze him or cause him to overcorrect. In the case of the former, he won't go all-in on his gift because "no" affirms he's not good enough, unworthy, and a victim. In the case of the latter, "no" causes him to overcorrect; they don't know—or perhaps care—that "no" means "no." He gets off by turning a "no" into a "yes" by selling customers things they don't need instead of selling

---

[13] Or perhaps I did and I just don't remember. In that case, amnesia is the real miracle.

himself on the one thing that would change everything—his novel, his screenplay, his album.

In either case, he becomes a great salesmen, selling himself a lifetime supply of self-sabotage—and his commission is Default.

Default and "Love"

I was sexually abused several times before my teenage years.

I wasn't going to include this, because it was a pretty jacked up situation. Then I thought about it, and what's really jacked up is: who *hasn't?* That's tongue-in-cheek. Many haven't experienced sexual abuse, and thank God for that. And I'm in no way mitigating sexual abuse toward children. I'm simply advocating my honest disclosure and cultural awareness, and because of that, it was an easy decision to include this in the book, no matter how sobering it might be.

Anyway, I wouldn't say I hit puberty early, but I always, for as long as I can remember, had an unquenchable, almost lustful desire for sex.

I'm serious.

It probably had something to do with my earlier years, but I had a strong want for intimacy at an early age. I'm talking third grade, man.

So, when the opportunity presented itself with an older kid—someone within the family, as is usually the case, sadly enough—I just let it happen.

What was I supposed to do?

He was giving me something I wanted, something I desired.

Was it love?

Was it favor?

It felt like it.

I didn't know any better.

Default loves it when we don't know any better, because then we just, as I said, let it happen.

Default and Story—Part Two

"Open up your accordion folders, take out a piece of looseleaf and—" my fifth-grade teacher, Mrs. Schmitz said, swinging a look over her shoulder at the clock above the whiteboard. "For the next forty-five minutes or so," she said, looking back at me and my classmates. "Write a story. Whatever comes to you."

Only eleven years old, I had never written a story before. But for whatever reason, I took to it like a moth to a flame. The time flew by. What I wrote carried me away.

Forty-five minutes later. I nodded affirmingly to myself, setting my pencil down in the concave slot at the top of my desk. I grabbed my graphite-smudged piece of looseleaf and strutted toward Mrs. Schmitz.

I don't remember what I wrote, but it must have been good.

A minute or so into reading my story, her shoulders started to bounce with silent laughter. She fingered tears from her eyes, looking at me with parentheses at the corners of her mouth. "It's just so funny!"

There I was, a fifth-grade boy who'd just made a grown-up laugh and cry with nothing but words on a page.

The praise felt good, but only for a moment. My buddies weren't writers. They were athletes. They were popular with the girls.

My mom shopped for me in the husky section at The Gap. I tried my best as a goalie in soccer, standing in front of the net praying the ball wouldn't get by me. When it came time for the annual fitness test in gym class, I couldn't do a single push-up or chin-up to save my life. I came in dead last in the mile run. But hey, I did have something my buddies didn't—a binder full of *Pokémon* and *Yu-Gi-Oh!* cards.

That was the day I knew I was a writer. Sadly, that was also the day I put down the pencil, so to speak, and began a self-sabotaging spree.

I wanted what my eleven-year-old head thought was success.

Girls.

Status.

Athletics and aesthetics.

I started chasing those things; sprinting toward the ways of the world instead of words.

Instead of writing whatever came to me, I let Default try and rewrite what had already been written.

The Beginning of the End

My mom and Andy divorced in 2004.

I was thirteen, going on fourteen years old.

I was also elated, for two reasons.

- Their seven-year-gong-show-of-a-marriage was finally over. That's my perspective on their marriage by the way, not theirs. It's cliché, but perception is reality, and I lay in bed on hundreds of nights praying they would get divorced. Kids don't pray for things like that if their reality doesn't warrant it.
- Secondly, I figured that meant I could see my dad again. I pitched the idea to my mom.

She accepted, on one condition: that Chuck, my psychiatrist, mediate our reunion in his office. Again, probably a smart move by my mom—I hadn't seen my dad in nearly a decade.

It was like meeting a stranger.

After several weekly meetings with the three of us, office visits became afternoon hangouts at my dad's apartment on the outskirts of Green Bay.

One of those afternoons involved a game of HORSE at the local park down the street.

My dad had an H and an O when I drained a three-pointer.

I passed him the ball.

He missed badly.

"Ha!" I said, gathering the rebound. "Now you're a HOR!"

I laughed.

He didn't.

He couldn't.

"Dad?" I said.

He pulled his hoodie over his head. "I'm gonna have one of my moments," he said, putting his hands on his knees, wobbling around like a badly controlled puppet.

Only thirteen at the time, I thought he was just goofing off. I jumped on his back.

Down he went.

Panicked, I rolled him onto his back.

His eyes were doll-like and glassy.

He was drooling.

My dad brought a shaky finger to his lips. "I'm havinguhseesure," he said, leering at me. "Thas why I'm talking like a reeethard."

A few moments later, the seizure escaped him.

Seizures weren't an uncommon occurrence for my dad—having a brain tumor will do that to you. He had surgery to remove the tumor when I was still in his life as a toddler, but remnants still remained.

The occasional seizure was something he learned to live with. Suffice to say, my dad's brain tumor was under control, kind of.

But not anymore.

That seizure was different. I don't think either of us knew it then, but that wasn't the beginning for him and me. It was the beginning of the end.

The Way—Part Two

After our game of HORSE, my dad had two surgeries in six months to remove the brain tumor.

Each surgery was more aggressive than the last. Each surgery, we were told, was a success—if by *success* you mean pissing off the tumor. The tumor came back with a vengeance each time; bigger and stronger, leaving my dad on death's door in the summer of 2005.

I was fourteen at the time. I was about to be a freshman in high school. I spent a great deal of time in the weight room. I was getting ready to play football that fall—a sport I hadn't played since fifth grade,[14] right around the time I stopped writing.

One night, after attending a Donald Driver football camp, I brought my dad a football autographed by Driver himself.

Driver was my dad's favorite player.

"I promise you, dad," I said, placing the ball on his lap. "I'm going to make it to the NFL."

My dad fluttered his lips and rolled his eyes. He couldn't speak at that point, his body had resigned from his rapid decline. Some might find it cruel of a father to dismiss his son's dream, but I don't believe that's what my dad was

[14] Yeah, I played football the summer going into fifth grade. It was a disaster. Hence, why I didn't play again until high school.

doing. I believe he was effectively saying, "If you only knew what you were truly capable of, football would pale in comparison. I can't wait for the day you see how incredible you really are."

That's when it happened.

My dad fluttered his lips again. A jet of air escaped him. His eyes went wide with cat-like fervor.

"Dad?" I said, placing my hand on his. His skin was slick with scare-sweat. His chest rose and fell like an accordion. *"Dad?"*

He wouldn't look at me. His eyes were trained on the corner of the living room, directly over my shoulder. It was a tiny, obscure space.

A narrow gate, if you will.

What is he looking at? I thought, swinging a look over my shoulder.

Nothing but beige.

"Dad?" I said, thumbing behind me. "Is—" I swallowed hard, trying to reckon with myself before asking a question that'd make me feel like a Looney Tune. "Is someone over there?"

My dad nodded. His face went white as a sheet.

My breath caught as if on a thorn. I was even more hesitant to ask the following question, but having gone to private school my whole life, I was out of guesses.

"Is it Jesus?"

My dad nodded again, this time with as much strength as I'd seen since our game of HORSE.

When my dad was weak, *He* was strong.

I didn't say or ask anything else after that. My dad's gaze didn't leave that corner for several minutes. I figured Jesus was comforting him. I wasn't about to get in His way.

I knew it was over when my dad's eyes found mine.

He just looked at me, his eyes welling.

I didn't know why.

Maybe I wasn't supposed to?

The Way—Part Three

September 5, 2005

It was a Monday night, just my second week in high school.

My dad was fading fast.

"I'd be surprised if he makes it past midnight," the hospice nurse said, sitting beside my dad while he lay on the bed in his living room. She frowned, unwrapping the stethoscope around her neck, checking his heartbeat. She shook her head and said: "He's very weak."

She wasn't kidding. I'd watched him go from being Herculean and carved out of stone, to nothing but a skin-sleeve covered in bed sores. Each breath for him was a battle in itself. It sounded like my dad's throat was covered with 60-grit sandpaper and some sadistic soul was striking matches against it.

As I said, he was fading fast.

"I'd suggest getting anyone who wants to be here when—" the nurse cut herself short with morbid neatness, then continued: "Well, you know."

An hour later, two yellow cones of light swept through the living room. My mom pulled into the driveway. I pushed myself to my feet, rounded the edge of my dad's hospital bed, kissed him on the forehead and said: "Love you dad."

When I was halfway out the front door, I swung a look over my shoulder and said: "See you tomorrow."

I was caught between teenage naivete and an ultra-yearning for sympathy. One part of me thought my dad wasn't going anywhere. The other part of me—a much larger part of me—knew he was going to die that night and was looking forward to the attention I'd get after the fact.

That's Default.

It was like my heart had been hardened into granite. It was like, in some perverse way, I was preparing to rejoice in my own misfortune because that was my story.

I was taken from my dad as a toddler.

Now he'd be taken from me as a teenager.

That made sense to me.

I was a victim.

That was my story.

Half an hour later I was lying on my bed, eyes peeled and locked on the ceiling waiting for the—

My phone rang.

"Hello?" I said.

"Hunter," it was my dad's girlfriend, Karen. "Hunter, your dad is gone."

My dad didn't want me there when he went to be with Jesus.

I made sure of that, but why?

Maybe because I was supposed to write about it someday?

Default and Addiction—Part One

"Sorry to hear about your dad," my friends told me the next day at school. "Real sorry, Hunt."

I shrugged my shoulders. "Sh** happens," I said.

I stuffed my pain and anger and frustration down. I had thoughts coming out of my pores. I had questions. I also had the answer, writing, but at that point in my life, I forgot I had that gift.

In sterquilinus invenitur.

To deal with everything I was going through, I started cutting instead. Sadly, like sexual abuse, most kids experience—or experiment—with this particularly secretive form of self-mutilation.

I was one of those kids—except for the secretive part.

During my freshman year, I'd go into my closet most days after school. In there, I'd straighten out a wire clothes hanger and slash my forearms.

"I went up north this weekend," I told my friends when they'd ask me about the bloody hashtags from my wrists to my elbows. "I ran through a bunch of pricker-bushes."

I made the, dare I say, rookie mistake of slashing the outside of my forearms instead of the inside. Harder to keep it a secret when everyone saw it. Maybe, at least subconsciously, I didn't want it to be a secret? I was a victim, right?

I was addicted to being afflicted.
I was addicted to being myself.

Default and Addiction—Part Two

I eventually stopped cutting.

But, like most addicts, I went from one self-sabotaging activity to another.

Default is a Hydra.

I put down the wire clothes hanger and picked up what I thought was success—building my body into a One-Man Wrecking Crew on the football field (I had a promise to keep to my dad about making it to the NFL, didn't I?) and becoming ultra-popular, especially with the girls.

That was success to me.

After my senior season in the fall of 2008, my prowess on the football field earned me a scholarship to play football at St. Cloud State University. And thank God for that, for reasons that had nothing to do with football.

My roommate, Kyle Galik, was my best friend and more like a brother.

I clung to Kyle's dad, Bill, as if he were *my* dad.

My defensive line coach, Steve Grimit, was someone I wanted to be like in almost every way.

Those three guys changed my story.

Unfortunately, that change in narrative was brief. I would eventually be separated from all three of them one year later.

Why?

I was addicted to being afflicted.
I was addicted to being myself.

Be a Grimit—Part One

In December of 2009, after my freshman season at SCSU, my teammates and I were helping our coaches with an official visit for that spring's incoming recruiting class.

The itinerary was as follows:

- Have dinner with the recruit and his parents on campus.
- After dinner, the coaches would take the parents back to their hotels.
- My teammates and I would take the recruits back to the off-campus apartments and show them the time of their lives.

"They can't be drinking tonight," our head coach said. "No drinking, period! Are we clear?" That fall, our team had enough underage drinking violations to impair an entire naval fleet. The drunken debauchery cost us key players being suspended in games we would have won had they been available. Those losses cost us a playoff berth. So yeah, when it came time for the first official recruiting visit of the year, drinking was off the table.

Of course we didn't listen.

A few hours later, my recruit had to be taken to the hospital to have his stomach pumped.

The morning after I was sitting across from our head coach in his office.

"I've made the decision that you are no longer part of St. Cloud State's football team."

Coach Grimit vehemently disagreed with the head coach's decision.

I made a mistake, I own that.

Grimit knew that, too, but he must have seen something in me that was worth fighting for—something only he could see.

Something that had nothing to do with football.

Something redemptive.

Something meaningful.

Something that needed to get out of me, no matter how long it took.

Something like a story—my story, a story of transformation—even if it took another decade for me to change it and then write it.

Grimit knew it was in there; and it was worth fighting for.

That afternoon, Grimit and I sat in his office. I wiped my sweaty palms on my pant legs. He started dialing coaches across the country—he was pitching me to them—because if I were going to continue playing football, I needed to transfer.

"I don't want to leave you." I said, my eyes filling with water.

Grimit assured me everything was going to be okay. He transferred a handful of times during his playing days. "You're a phenomenal young man and you're going to have a great college football career."

I began to whimper, fighting to get the words out. Part of me thinks he knew what I was about to say, scooting his chair close to mine, waving me in for a fatherly embrace.

"You're the reason I committed to St. Cloud State." I said, burying my face into his red polo as he wrapped his arms around me.

That night my phone rang. It was the head coach at Grand Valley State.

A week later I worked out at the school, and then was

offered a scholarship.

Grimit gave me the chance to keep the promise I made to my dad.

Every man, self-sabotaging or not, needs a Grimit in his life.

And if you can't have a Grimit, then the next best thing is to be a Grimit.

Be the man who sees something in your friend, brother, coworker, *yourself,* and get it out of them—it's redemptive. It's their gift. It's worth fighting for.

Default and Transformation

My four years at Grand Valley State was a rerun of my time in high school—except for the self-mutilation part.

Well, kind of.

Instead of cutting, I became particularly fond of tattoos. Something about sitting on a bench, hunched over with my chest touching my thighs—for eight hours at a time—while a gentleman named Preston tattooed my entire back was oddly satisfying. To be clear, I'm not suggesting being tattooed is a form of self-sabotage. I just find it coincidental that the tattoo I got on my back in the summer of 2013 was a koi fish becoming a dragon.

A story of transformation.

A story every Self-Sabotaging Man—and all of mankind, for that matter—knows, even if he doesn't know he knows it.

It's primordial.

It's archetypal.

It's The Way out of self-sabotage and into self-mastery.

I wasn't concerned about that, and I sure as hell wasn't concerned with writing. Like my dad the night he died, my writing was in a desiccated state; hoping and praying to be saved, revivified, transformed from the decayed derelict it had become into the gift from God it was meant to be.

Self-Sabotage on Steroids

I didn't make it to the NFL.

Despite Grimit's faith in me, I didn't have a phenomenal college football career. Just an average one, ending in December of 2013. Alas, with football in the rearview mirror, trying to start my life as a professional instead of an athlete when deep down I knew I was actually a writer was weird.

From May 2014 to January 2016, I worked at a private training facility in Grand Rapids. I trained adults in the morning, kids in the evening. I didn't mind split-shifts, the owner appreciated it. He gave me three raises in my first year. He had big plans for me.

On my twenty-fifth birthday, he gave me a copy of *The War of Art* by Steven Pressfield.

Inside the front cover he wrote:

> *To one of the most unique and charismatic individuals I know on his 25th birthday, continue to face and beat the challenger 'Resistance.'*
>
> *Your growth in this life is infinite. It knows no limit.*
>
> *Use your many talents, gifts, and aspirations for the Glory of God.*
>
> *Keep developing into a*

Pro.

Flow like water.

Always a white belt.

You're an All-Star teammate, friend, and person.

People are drawn to you—don't waste the opportunity to impact.

Thank you for the year of 24.

Aim high for 25.

Everyone eats.

Few hunt.

- Mark

(sorry for the smudges—chubby hands...)

I left his facility six weeks later, starting my own gym in a pole barn in the spring of 2016. I should have stayed at his gym, taking that time between shifts to go all-in on writing.

That felt *meh* to me.

What felt better was affirming my victimhood because he was paying me twenty-five bucks an hour when he said he wanted to pay me forty an hour—but in order to do so he'd have to fire someone.

So, I said to hell with it and became his competitor.

My gym's training philosophy was focused on speed development. That played well in the market. We went from a couple clients and a squat rack in a pole barn to over one hundred athletes inside a commercial suite in ten months. I poached several of his athletes—one of them became my girlfriend, another a mentee and friend, Thomas—taking them on as clients and staff at my gym. People were drawn to me, right?

I was killing it, but something was missing.

Having not played football in nearly three years, I wanted to fill that athletic absence in my life. I needed to fill that void. I had practically lived in the weightroom since my freshman year of high school. So, I tried powerlifting.

I did a deadlift-only meet in August of 2016.

I loved it, and I was good at it.

Wanting to see how good I could get, I started taking steroids.

Beating Resistance wasn't a problem for me. From the time I left my boss' gym to the fall of 2017, I had been published twice in periodicals (seeing my name on the covers at Barnes & Noble was cool, I won't lie). I was named *Simplifaster's* "Favorite Contributor of the Year" in 2017. I was gaining notoriety in the strength and conditioning industry.

I could beat Resistance, but I couldn't beat myself.

It was like self-sabotage on steroids.

Oh wait.

#SPRINTORDIE—Part One

In October 2017, after a six-month, five-compound steroid cycle,[15] I won my first powerlifting championship—and then quit my powerlifting career half an hour later.

It was another meaningless win, another successful self-sabotaging activity.

I remember looking at myself in the mirror in the men's room. I had my first-place medal around my neck, plaque in my right hand. My face was swollen, having ballooned to almost three hundred pounds from the steroid cycle leading up to the meet. My thighs were caked with chalk.

What're you doing? I thought, looking at my reflection in disgust. *You own a gym that prides itself on speed. Look at you. You can't even jump over a ruler. Much less, book it ten yards without blowing out your calf.*

I sent a Facebook message to a friend.

"Derek," I said. "I need your help. If I'm going to be the best (speed) coach I can be, then I need to be *doing* it."

Derek had experience in sprint-training considerations for non-track athletes—including NFL offensive and defensive lineman—and he was intrigued at the prospect of training me, seeing as though I had a similar build.

---

[15] For the record, steroids are illegal. They're not "legal" in powerlifting; they're just not tested for. A strange kind of willful blindness, I know.

"Let's document everything on social media," he responded, then continued: "This will be interesting."

Oh, it was interesting all right. It's not every day you see a near-three-hundred-pound powerlifter sprinting down a track. I ran as smooth as a car with square wheels.

But as time went on, I got better, smoother, leaner.

My body transformed, losing over thirty pounds in three months. Too bad the transformation was only physical.

By the spring of 2018, my notoriety and reach on the internet was growing. I was consulting with athletes in Australia. I was on podcasts every other week. I gave Thomas the reins at my gym as Director of Operations. I was traveling the country. I had my own hashtag on Instagram: #SPRINTORDIE. I wrote numerous articles on *Simplifaster.* I was experiencing so much success, I started another business: Charneski Power Coaching & Consulting—a shadow career—and Default was off and running.

The Way—Part Four

The summer of 2018 is a time I'll never forget—an All is Lost Moment followed by an Epiphanal Moment.

As promising as my profession was, my personal life was perverse. If I wasn't blind to my own self-sabotage, then I was exaggerating life's adversities to keep myself a slave to self-sabotaging activities: cocaine, acid, steroids, money, status, women, the works. I was dating up to three women at a time; and my girlfriend knew it, God bless her. She was one tough cookie; but a woman can only take so much before she breaks.

One night she didn't break, she shattered.

"Do you remember the time I went to California after your powerlifting meet last fall?" she said.

"Yeah," I said. "Why?"

"Well," she said. "A few weeks after I got home, I found out I was pregnant."

My mind raced. It was June. When she found out she was pregnant it would have been Halloween at the latest. She wasn't showing at all. That could only mean—

"You had an abortion?"

She was weeping now. "We weren't ready."

"Okay," I said.

There was a pause on the other end of the line. "I—" she said, sounding relieved. "I didn't think that's how you'd respond."

I guess it didn't sink in until later on. In the moment I shrugged it off with the same laissez faire attitude the night my dad died. Instead of allowing myself to feel for her or face the reality that I should have been a father—maybe she would have given me a son? What a story that would have been; to be for him what I longed for all my life—a dad. Instead, I chose to not feel anything at all. In some weird way, it worked. It fit my inner narrative. That story made sense to me. I was under the dominion of Default—a slave to my own self-sabotage—and I was literally destroying lives in the process.

I was the victim and the villain.

Speaking of parents, less than a month later I met someone.

Thomas needed my help one day at the gym. I obliged him, making myself available to conduct an intake interview with a prospective athlete and his mother.

I remember setting the paperwork down on a bench when I looked up and there she was. A slender brunette stood in the sunlight at the end of our gym's garage. She had big sunglasses on, holey jeans and flip-flops. I was frozen with fire, like an empty vase filled with liquid sunlight.

"Tiffany," she said, offering me her hand. "Nice to meet you."

"You as well." I said, accepting her hand, pumping it twice.

Her eyebrows lifted. "And your name?"

"Oh." I cleared my throat. "Hunter."

A smile touched the corners of her mouth, then she placed a hand on the young man's shoulder next to her. "And this is my son, Sam."

Sam was thirteen, going on fourteen years old and without a father.

Here's your chance, some voice called out from the nosebleed seats in the back of my mind. *Be for him what you've longed for all your life—a dad.*

Life is funny, isn't it?

Sam signed up for my gym that day.

Tiffany and I were dating shortly after.

This Isn't Fun Anymore

October 2018

Bass.

I could hear bass.

The kind of bass that gets your blood moving.

The kind of bass that gets your heart pumping.

The kind of bass that made me *see* sound as I was up to my eyes in acid, cocaine, booze, and God only knows what else.

It was a little after one in the morning. I remember sitting on a white sofa in the VIP corner of a nightclub in downtown Grand Rapids. My sweat-soaked shirt clung to my chest.

I remember staring at a *RESERVED FOR HUNTER CHARNESKI* sign on the drinks table in front of me. A chrome bowl big enough to bathe a toddler idled on top of it; it was filled with bottles of liquor atop ice that looked like a king's ransom of crushed diamonds.

I remember gazing out at the dimly lit dance floor. The fifty or so people on it didn't look like people at all, but a blended, purplish-blue spirit swaying with the music like a steamy tendril.

I pressed my eyes shut. But that didn't keep me from seeing things. What I saw when I closed my eyes was much worse.

I saw hell.

I was in an elevator, plunging down to the cellar of my soul. When I reached the bottom—though it didn't feel like the bottom at all, it felt like I could keep going down forever—there I was. But it wasn't me as I was then. It was me as a little boy. A little boy who'd been told "no" for the last time. He wasn't in a closet, he was in a cell. He was wailing. Torrents of tears streamed down his cheeks, making the orange in his hazel eyes bright like hellfire. He was rattling the bars of his cell, begging to be let out—begging *me* to let him out.

I opened my eyes. The bass matched my heartbeat, a padded hammer behind my sternum. I fished my phone out of my pocket, dialing my ex.

Why didn't I call Tiffany?

We'd only been together a couple months. I was afraid this sort of thing would scare her off, or at least that's what I told myself. The real reason I didn't call Tiffany is because she was my present, and potential future—both of which I didn't know.

What I didn't know scared me.

My ex, by definition, was a representation of my past—something I knew too well.

"Hello?" my ex answered groggily.

I closed my eyes again. When I did, my vision turned kaleidoscopic. It was like being hurled through the Bifrost in Marvel's *Thor* movies. Being taken up from hell to heaven—which might've been worse than hell.

What I saw next was what could have been.

I landed in an office.

It was *my* office.

There was a bookshelf in the corner, filled with books, both fiction and non. But there weren't the usual suspects in it. No books by Stephen King, Steven Pressfield, Anne Rice, or other literary greats. All the books had a different name, my name, on their spine.

Then I heard the little boy again, crying out from the

sepulcher of my spirit.

"He gave you the words," he said, his cry echoing in my head. "But you never wrote! You never wrote! You never wrote! You never—"

"Hunter?" My ex said again. "*Hunter?*"

I got slammed back to the white sofa.

I dragged a hand down my tear-streaked cheeks, shook my head and said: "This isn't fun anymore."

I don't remember what happened after that.

Next thing I knew, I was staring at my reflection in the men's room. The man looking back at me died a long time ago, he just didn't know it yet. He had cracks in his cheeks, like his face was made of weathered stone. Those little cracks became yawning chasms, wide enough for spirits to slither inside, filling him with another person entirely. That person was possessed to wander aimlessly through the wilderness. That person was possessed by pointless pursuits of money, sex, status, meaningless wins, idols and coaches and mentors.

Then I looked into my eyes.

Oh God, my eyes.

They were as black as fish eggs. Inside each eye was that little boy again. He was helplessly clanging against his cell as it sank into a black lake, each its own separate and particular hell.

I gripped the porcelain sink and closed my eyes.

Bass.

I could hear bass.

#SPRINTORDIE—Part Two

February 2019

Fifteen months after my first sprint, I competed in my first track meet. The meet was at my alma mater, Grand Valley State, where I played football. The meet wasn't open,[16] it was an NCAA meet.[17] Meaning, I'd be racing against collegiate sprinters—kids who were more than one hundred pounds lighter than me—most of whom had been sprinting for fifteen years, not fifteen months.

I ran the sixty-meter dash in 7.58 seconds.

Not world class by any stretch of the imagination. But not bad for a guy who, at the time, weighed 257 pounds—and I didn't come in last. I edged out some poor kid from Cornerstone University at the finish line. I posted the race footage later that day. You can imagine how social media reacted to such a physical feat.

Talk about a Gateway Drug for Default, dear God.

Over the course of the next six months:

---

[16] Open track meets are, as the name implies, open to everyone.

[17] You might be wondering *how in the heck did they let you into an NCAA meet?* And fair enough. When registering online, the form asks what you predict to run in the event you're competing in. I asked Derek; he had me put in a time he deemed acceptable, (7.63 seconds). Not a bad guess, eh?

I wrote two ebooks, one a simple speed system, the other a tad more complex, both proprietary. Both led to presentations, keynote speeches, and consultations across the country. I put together an online #SPRINTORDIE Masterclass through a private Facebook group. I had back-to-back five-figure coaching appointments, one at my training facility in Michigan and another at the client's gigantic training complex in the hills of Eugene, Oregon (you should have seen the mountain lion tracks, man). I became a physical rehab expert, expediting the recovery time for strained hamstrings and calves (ten days for the former, inside of three weeks for the latter). I made enough money in that time to put a down payment on a condo in Arizona and give my gym away.

And I did.

Necessary Failure

Michelangelo's *La Pieta* is a sculpture of Mother Mary holding her son, Jesus, broken and destroyed in her arms after He was taken down from the cross.

That's just the external story of Michelangelo's sculpture.

The internal story for Mother Mary, and every mother, is far deeper.

Perhaps the most difficult thing a mother will ever do in her life is to voluntarily offer her son to the Big Bad World so he can fall—so he can fail. It's a necessary failure so he can become the man he needs to, and she's the one to facilitate it.

Brutal.

"I'm moving to Arizona," I said to Tiffany in the summer of 2019, holding her hands in mine as we sat on her living room couch.

She frowned, then said: "Where does that leave us?"

"I don't know," I said, sighing.

Tiffany followed with a sigh of her own. Her eyes went downcast, seemingly searching the carpet for an answer. She must have found one. "Do what you need to do," she said, sniffling. "I think you need to go."

I'm not comparing Tiffany to Mother Mary, nor me to

Jesus Christ, but the analogy is glaringly obvious. Tiffany not only had to let me go die, so to speak, but she also had to facilitate it.

She knew I had to wander aimlessly in the wilderness.

She knew I needed to fail.

It was necessary.

Paying It Backward—Part One

A few days later, I took Thomas out to dinner.

He thought we were just grabbing a bite to eat, which wasn't out of the norm. He and I had eaten out dozens of times since he came to work for me. But at that point, he and I were more than boss and employee—we were best friends. In Thomas' mind, I'm sure he thought that was just another dinner with his homie.

Not quite.

He had no idea just how full his plate was about to be.

"I'll be back in just a sec with some water," our waitress said as Thomas and I slid in our booth.

We nodded our thanks. Then I plucked a tri-folded letter from my breast pocket, pushing it across the table toward him.

"What is this?" Thomas said, placing a hand over the letter.

I shifted my eyes from his to the letter and offered a subtle nod, cuing him to see for himself.

Thomas opened the letter.

His eyes widened.

And no wonder.

The letter effectively said:

> *Sign on the dotted line and I, Hunter Michael Charneski, shall relinquish one hundred percent of my business' shares to you,*

Thomas So-and-So.

Thomas squinted hard, then cleared his throat and said: "Why are you doing this?"

"Well—"

"And don't tell me you're just paying it forward."[18]

"Because you're worth it, Thomas," I said, smiling. "Because you're worth it."

Since running in my first meet, I was gaining exposure and notoriety in the industry as The Next Big Thing on all-things sprinting.

Wanting more success, I figured the only logical thing to do was to go somewhere I could train, coach, and consult on all-things sprinting—every day if I wanted to.

The idea of moving to Arizona, and the prospect of the success and notoriety I could attain when I got there, made me not want my gym anymore. So, I tried selling it, which proved to be a fool's errand.

The business' evaluator deemed it worthless without me.

This enraged me.

Sure, the gym was beyond profitable, but the thing was like a baby who never grew up and always needed to be fed. The only way I was going to be able to leave it all behind and jettison to Arizona would be by dumping the whole thing on Thomas' plate.

So, I did.

I, like my gym, was a baby who never grew up and always needed to be fed.

Thomas was right. I wasn't paying it forward—that would have involved doing something kind for someone else without expecting anything in return. But I *was* expecting something in return. I was expecting a twenty-three-year-old

---

[18] Paying it forward was one of my gym's Core Values.

kid to sign on the dotted line so I could run away from responsibility; from the unconditional love Tiffany and her son Sam gave me; from the prospect of having a steady and stable relationship with her, and the chance to be the father for Sam I never had; so, I could affirm my victimhood. That was my story.

Thomas signed.

Giving that gym away was the most selfish thing I've ever done.

It was deceit disguised as nobility.

That's how Default works.

It pathologized me into believing I was philanthropic when really, I was just psychopathic—I was the victim and the villain.

I wasn't paying it forward. I was paying it backward.

The Letter

I got to Phoenix on September 5, 2019.

Business was great.

I consulted with a couple NFL teams for return-to-play protocols on hamstrings and calves, as well as sprint training considerations for linemen—since I was close to three hundred pounds when I started sprinting.

I was hired for multiple high-ticket training appointments. I started a podcast, #SPRINTORDIE Radio, and it was gaining traction. The move to Arizona was a success, and so was I.

That was the problem.

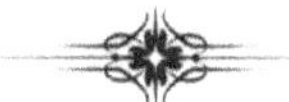

By February 2020, Tiffany had visited a few times, Thomas only once.

Thomas saw all he needed to, and it wasn't good.

He saw me cheat on Tiffany.

He saw me cheat on Sam.

He told them both what he'd seen.

"Disgraceful," was what Tiffany called me, and she was right.

After that, I was alone. I had yet again, pushed out everyone in my life who did nothing but love me.

I was the victim and the villain.

I was like the Israelites, alone in the desert, wandering in the wilderness.

Then one morning, I opened my email and found a note from Thomas.

The subject line read: *I am worried about you.*

> *Hunter,*
>
> *I want to frame this first by saying I don't want to do this. This is going to hurt. It's going to hurt you and it's equally going to hurt me. I am at fault for a lot of things and I want to apologize for not doing this sooner but this is a necessary step in repairing our severely broken relationship.*

Severely broken relationship? I thought.

> *When I first met you, you were exactly what I needed at that time in my life. You taught me so much. But you also believed in me, which is something I had never experienced. I will always be grateful and appreciative for that. But where I went wrong is **I made you my idol**. Rather than looking to you for guidance, I took every word you said as gospel truth and wrapped my identity in your approval and how similar I could be to you.*

Yeah, I thought. *And? Seems to have worked out for you so far….*

> *This may not seem like the worst thing in the world, but ultimately this led me into a downward spiral of deceit and forced me to be someone I was not comfortable with nor who I wanted to be. I believed that in order to be successful I had to be as much like you as I could (again my fault) and that there was no other way to make it.*

Okay you lost me. I thought. *You're my greatest accomplishment there, buddy. What's the problem?*

> *This led me to stuff down a lot of things that I should have been truthful about or called you out on, but I was too afraid of your reaction/opinion of me. A lot of bitterness developed, but again, shame on me for being afraid and not speaking the truth. The truth is, I've disagreed with you on most things since we met.*

Oh.

> *I know you are unhappy,*

> *I know you're not in a good spot, but you know why. No one can help you unless you help yourself. You've done a very good job of bringing very giving and sympathetic people into your life, but people can only give so much without getting anything in return. Your world feels like it's caving in because all the people closest to you are leaving, and I know you've thought about why.*

At this point I was upset, anger was near. I was angry because Thomas was right. I had thought about why.

> *The truth is, you are an extremely selfish person...but we all are.*

An extremely selfish *person?* My face felt hot. *This dude's awfully quick to forget the fact that I gave him my gym for Chrissake!*

> *But anytime people are around you they are walking on eggshells because it's Hunter's way or else. It never starts that way, but it always gets to that stage at some point.*

He hit the nail right on the head. My mom once told my ex: "When you get involved with Hunter, you're being invited into *his* world; you're part of *his* world. That's just the way he is."

> *If you're not ready to be honest with yourself, I get it. But until you put the opinion of others, your training, and your business to the side and get some professional help, nothing will change and you will continue to feel empty and purposeless.*
>
> *I know I cannot control your reaction to this letter. And should you choose to receive this through any other lens than that of love, that's on you.*

Thomas was urging me to change my story.

> *You know it would have been easier for me to just cut ties and say nothing at all, so I hope you realize how much I do care about you. You are on my heart and mind constantly and I pray for you daily.*
>
> *Love,*
> *Thomas*

I didn't want to accept that Thomas was right.

But I could accept trying to find a way out of the wilderness.

I started therapy the next week.

More Than Okay

April 2020

I called Tiffany. We hadn't spoken in a few months.

"You sound different," she said.

I shrugged, pacing my balcony, looking at Camelback Mountain in the distance. "I've been working really hard in therapy.[19] It's been way more work and way harder than I thought, but I know I need it."

"I know honey." *Honey?* I thought. "Well, you keep getting healthy and then, when you're ready, we'll be here."

"What do you mean?" I said, frowning.

"Once you've done what you need to do, once you're healthy, Sam and I will be here for you. When you're ready."

I couldn't help but laugh.

"What?"

I shrugged, wiping a sheen of sweat off my brow. "I think you ought to have your head examined."

"What?" Her tone was a trifle more stern, this time. "What's that supposed to mean?"

"Well," I scoffed. "What that means is, after all I've

---

[19] I did talk therapy. I learned what negative and positive cognitions were (i.e. the stories I was telling myself day in, day out) and the difference between the two. I became conscious of my unconscious thoughts—I started thinking about what I was thinking about. I did eye movement desensitization and reprocessing, (EMDR) which was a trip.

done to you and Sam, for you to say 'once I'm healthy again' that you two will be there to just…" I started talking with my hands now. "Welcome me back into your lives with open arms, then yeah, I think you ought to have your head examined." I said, then grunted. "I mean, why would you?"

"It's called *love,*" Tiffany said. "It's called *being a family*. I can't wait for the day when you see how incredible you really are."

I said nothing, my mouth went dry as chrome.

"Everything's gonna be okay," she said.

I sniffled, then choked through the word: "Yeah?"

"Mhmm," she said. "More than okay."

Write Your Book

Late May 2020

"Write your book," my therapist said at the end of our last session. "I can't wait to read it."

Fair enough. I thought. Sure, I self-sabotaged my gift of writing for several years, but I never lied to myself about the passion I had for it. I did love writing. Even then, I knew I had a book in me. I just never took the time to sit down and write the darn thing. But when my therapist told me to do just that, she didn't have to tell me twice.

It was literally the doctor's orders.

That was all fine and good, but I wasn't sure where to begin. So, I began where most stories do—in the beginning. What's more, it wasn't a shadow career. I was doing the kind of writing I was supposed to be doing.

No more blogging for notoriety's sake.

No more periodicals published at Barnes & Noble to pump my own tires.

No more dipping my toe in Writers' Water, if you will.

I went all-in.

Being a Family

Like all those years ago in Mrs. Schmitz's class, what I wrote carried me away—literally.

After learning more and more about myself the longer I sat in front of a Google Doc, I decided to reconcile with Tiffany and Sam.

I had done what I needed to do. But instead of Tiffany and Sam being there for me when I was ready, I was there for them.

I made a surprise visit to Michigan at the end of June, waiting for them when they got home from a baseball tournament.[20]

It's called *love.*

It's called *being a family.*

[20] I was in cahoots with Tiffany's stepmom, who gave me the garage code. I was waiting in the house when they got back.

Self-Realization—Part One

July 4, 2020

Tiffany, Sam, and I were on her parents' pontoon boat on Lake Isabella, just outside of Mount Pleasant, Michigan. The water was a midnight navy, tossing sunny winks off it.

It was a good time.

Then my phone vibrated. It was a Facebook message from an old high school friend, Hanna. I felt my mouth pull back and down, thinking: *the hell? Haven't talked to her in forever.*

Hanna's message read: "Did you see Jaide's post?"

Jaide was my best friend in high school. She was someone I could count on to pick me up during the hours God should have never made to get Taco Bell. She was someone who, during our senior year, vetted my girlfriend up, down, and around before giving her the thumbs up to date me. She was someone who, no matter what, would be there for me if I needed her.

And now she needed me.

I thumbed over to Instagram. When I did, my heart dropped faster than the phone from my hands. Jaide's husband overdosed on heroin the night before—leaving her with a ten-month-old, Andre, to raise on her own.

Hanna sent another message: "We're putting together a GoFundMe. Anything you can do to drive traffic to that page would be appreciated."

God must have been winding up since that day in Mrs. Schmitz's class, because an idea struck me like a bolt of lightning. *I'm going to write her a story.* I thought. *And I'll include a call to action for readers to donate!*

The GoFundMe had a $5K goal.

The story I wrote traveled faster than good news.

Within one week, the GoFundMe generated more than $25K—more than covering the funeral costs for Jaide and giving her some cushion as a newly single mom.

Talk about a *Deus Ex Machina*—and I mean that technically. One could wonder how 800 words generated that much money in so little time. And fair enough. The answer is the blog was really, really good. The *truth* is, it wasn't me who wrote it. It was divinely inspired—how could it have been otherwise?—I was just the instrument. I'm not dumb enough to take credit for words that weren't my own.

That story was different from a few tears and a chuckle from Mrs. Schmitz. What I wrote actually helped someone—someone I loved. What I wrote made money—more money than any shadow career or self-sabotaging activity ever did inside one week.

That was success, the kind of success I had been running from my entire life.

It was more than a success.

It was a moment of self-realization.

Be a Grimit—Part Two

Two weeks later, while still riding the high of helping Jaide, I got a text from a former teammate of mine at St. Cloud State.

"I was with Grimit last week. He still cares about you a lot. He was explaining your situation again and he said: 'The day they told me their decision on what to do with Hunter, was the only time I truly considered leaving the program. They completely mishandled his situation. I told them straight up, '*You're doing the wrong thing. This is a great person and he will do great things for this program and school.*'"

At that time, I was a hundred pages into my autobiography—a lead-in to this book, though indirect. In it, there were more than a couple chapters dedicated to Grimit; and the impact he had on my life. I couldn't wait to finish the book so he could read it and know how much he meant to me.

Sixteen days later, that same teammate sent me another text:

"Grimit passed away."

I felt heavier than a heart soaked in guilt.

Overcome with emotion and regret, I knew what I had to do. I had to do for him what I did for Jaide—tell a story, his story.

The goal of Grimit's story wasn't raising money. It was raising awareness—awareness of the type of individual

Steve Grimit was.

And that's exactly what it did.

At the time, it was the most shared piece of content I ever posted.[21] And no wonder. It made it painfully clear to readers that not everyone can be so lucky to have a guy like Grimit in their life, but they can most certainly *be* a Grimit.

They can see something in others; something others may not be able to see yet.

Something redemptive.

Something meaningful.

Something that needs to get out of them, no matter how long it takes.

Something like a story; a story of transformation.

What a gift that would be, and is—it's something worth fighting for.

Don't wait till tomorrow to help them change their story. And if the roles are reversed, as was the case with me, don't wait any longer to tell them how they helped you change your story. Don't wait till it's too late, like I did, and write about it.

Be about it.

Be a Grimit.

---

[21] It was written on my consulting business' website, which no longer exists. Grimit's story is in my own personal Google Docs.

The Disease of More—Part Two

August 2020

Beating Pressfield's Resistance only takes a moment.

Defeating Default takes more than a moment, it takes momentum.

Witnessing firsthand the waves those two stories created in as many weeks made me tune into a victim's favorite radio station—WIIFM (What's In It For Me?).

In my mind, a stupid autobiography wasn't going to make me a dime. So, I put it down and picked up another shadow career as a copywriter.

I made $10K my first week,[22] which was the worst thing that could have happened.

I wanted more.

---

[22] I'm sure anyone who's been in copywriting is wondering how one could make $10K in one week. The answer isn't sexy: I took a course, learned the X's and O's on how to write a Lead Generating PDF, a sales funnel, and the words on a website. From there, I Facebook messaged everyone on my Friends List (i.e. cold called), telling them what I could do for them. Out of the hundreds of folks I messaged, several responded, and one moved forward with the whole kit and kaboodle—all the services I listed above—which was a $10K investment. Like anything sales-related, it's just a numbers game.

The Kiss of Death

This is when things got really bad.

I was writing all the time—just not the kind of writing I should have been doing.

I was writing copy for email sales funnels, websites, and company one-liners.

Less than a month after marketing myself as a copywriter, my soul started to stir. I knew copywriting was just creating a copy of what I already was—a Self-Sabotaging Man.

My autobiography on the other hand was crappy, but it gave my soul solace, not suffering. However, solace didn't satisfy me. I wanted to become a better writer. So, I picked up *On Writing: A Memoir of the Craft* by one of the greatest writers of all-time, Stephen King.

For those who have read King's book, you're aware of the notorious *Writing Assignment.* For those who are not, King gives readers the parameters for a simple and short horror fiction story for them to write. No outline, either. Just five to six pages of letting, as Mrs. Schmitz said: "Whatever comes to you."

To hell with it, I thought. *Why not?*

A few hours later I had written my first horror story. It was called *The Kiss of Death.*

Aptly named, I must say.

Up until that point, the only piece of fiction I ever wrote was the story I placed on Mrs. Schmitz's desk nearly twenty years prior. I thought of myself as a nonfiction guy, through and through. But after completing King's *Writing Assignment,* I looked at Tiffany and said: "Not only do I think I like writing fiction, I think I like writing horror."

That was the kiss of death.

Not This Year

February 2021

I went back to Arizona at the end of September. With my newfound passion for horror, I submitted story after story—all of them were rejected. But they were rejected in a way that gave me hope.

> *"This is good,"* one rejection email read. *"Not what we're looking for, but it's good. I hope you find a home for it."*

That was the wrong thing to say to someone who was unconscious of their downward spiral of self-sabotage. I kept writing horror stories, trying my darndest to get that one acceptance letter.

I started my own publication on *Medium.*

I read *Letting Go: The Pathway to Surrender* by David R. Hawkins.

My condo was lit only by candles at night.

I meditated three hours per day.

I consulted crystals.

I tried everything.

I was in another realm, man.

I had my mind made up. I wasn't going to do anything else but write. I was alone in the desert for Chrissake—what else was I going to do? I tried writing my first novel: *A*

Werewolf Story until I went broke five months later and had to ask my mom for money.

"I don't know how else to say this," I said to my mother, sitting on an eggshell-white sofa across from me. I clasped my hands together and shrugged. "I've got forty-four dollars to my name."

I had everything I could have wanted, and more, and it wasn't enough. I imagine God folded His arms and shook His head at me in disappointment. I imagine He threw His hands up, just like when the Israelites complained about manna instead of meat, and then gave me all the "meat" I could handle.

Then the "plague" came—in the desert, at that—just like the Israelites.

I couldn't get a remote coaching client if I trained them for free.

Forget copywriting. The one $10K client was a fluke. The only other job I got was writing copy for a women's jewelry company—which didn't last long. As for online consulting and private Facebook courses, my audience knew me as #SPRINTORDIE and when my business stopped showing me sprinting, it died.

Eventually I got my business running again, which led to becoming head strength coach for Phoenix's Indoor Football League team, the Arizona Rattlers.

Then things happened fast.

I sold my condo that September, Tiffany sold her house in West Michigan.

We bought a new house in Georgetown Township, Michigan.

On a layover in Minneapolis, I got an email. It was from the editor of an Australian horror fiction publisher. They accepted my story titled: *Not This Year* I submitted one month prior for their upcoming Halloween special.

I was out of the desert, but I was still wandering in the wilderness.

I wasn't going to stop sabotaging myself, not this year.
Default is as much mental as it is environmental.
Wherever I went, there I was.

A New Default—Part Two

May 2022

Moving back to Michigan was good.

Not having a job when I got there was not so good.

Don't get me wrong, I did enough to meet my half of the expenses as a freelance copywriter, but I was struggling to find a stable job.

I hired a sales coach—more like Tiffany hired a sales coach, since I used her credit card.

He was a smart guy. I liked him. He *loved* me, probably because I took everything he said as if it was the Word of God.

What was I selling? Not copywriting, but as—get this—a personal development coach.

That's hilarious.

My product was called *Artistic Warrior*—a cohort for creative alpha males who are successfully stuck; who want to find the way out of self-sabotage and into self-mastery.

It didn't last long.

Artistic Warrior, like *A Werewolf Story,* was too big for me. I wasn't ready for either. I needed to become an Artistic Warrior first. I needed to undergo my own lycan-like transformation before I could even think about writing a story that's truly scary.

One morning while perusing LinkedIn, I saw a job opening as an Insurance Agent at a financial firm in downtown Grand Rapids.

My sales coach loved insurance.

He told me to push an application.

He told me I had the chops for it.

I applied that day.

My phone rang twenty minutes later. It was one of the Partners in the office, John was his name.

I toured the office forty-eight hours later. I liked it. The idea of strolling around the cubicles in a suit everyday felt oddly right. I liked the prospect of working in an office—something I'd never done before—it made the adult-aged adolescent in me feel like a grown up, I think. And I really liked John, we gelled immediately.

My first day at the firm was May 16, and though I didn't know it yet, that was the beginning of the long and painful end of Default.

I was about to find The Way out of self-sabotage and into self-mastery.

PART TWO: REDEFINING DEFAULT

"I am the way and the truth and the life. No one comes to the Father except through me." – John 14:6

60. Overture

Part Two is a hero's journey—a *documented* hero's journey.

During my time in Michigan in the summer of 2020 (after writing the blogs for Jaide and Grimit, but sometime before I began writing fiction) I came across the hero's journey—perhaps the oldest form of storytelling.

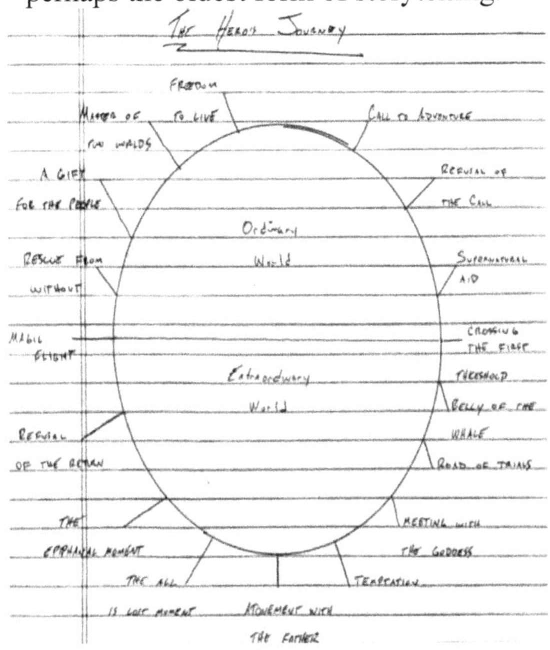

Image 3: My wonderfully artistic representation of the Hero's Journey, source: The Hero With A Thousand Faces by Joseph Campbell

I don't remember exactly how the concept of the hero's journey was introduced to me, and I don't think it matters. What matters is, the more I studied the hero's journey, the more I connected with it. It was a deep, meaningful, almost intimate connection—practically symbiotic, really. I was able to piece parts of my life—chapters, you might say—in perfect sequence that followed the steps laid out in the image above.

It was uncanny.

I started looking at life differently. It made sense to me. What's more, I couldn't see my life through any other lens after that. Just ask my wife. Life happened just like the way it does in the movies.

Take the summer of 2018 for example. My ex called me and by the end of our conversation, I realized I was the very thing that stopped me from becoming a dad—the victim and the villain. My All is Lost Moment. Weeks later I met Tiffany and her son, Sam. Sam, who was my age when I lost my dad, was fatherless. Was that a coincidence? Or was it the hero's journey coinciding with my life for what was the Epiphanal Moment?

That's just a snippet from a single story inside that particular hero's journey. I could go on and on with other examples from previous hero's journeys,[23] but that's not important. What is important is that—and I'm sure you're already making connections from your own life to the hero's journey—your life is a story. And if you're anything like me, then perhaps our stories aren't so different.

To illustrate that point, Part Two is the story of how I finally, after twenty years, burned the Golden Calf my Default made my deity; how I put God first, went all-in on

---

[23] If you read this book more than once, you'll notice the patterns of the hero's journey in Part One.

my gift of writing, and am now running *my* race, not someone else's.

Part Two's hero's journey lasted 308 days. It began on July 7, 2022, and ended on May 11, 2023. In the introduction I said it's *documented,* which might be a misnomer. That gives the impression I was recording each stage in real time. That's not how the hero's journey works. There are too many factors at play simultaneously to be fully present and aware of what stage you're in as it's happening.

A better way to describe the hero's journey in Part Two might be *circumstantial,* or better yet, *learned.* I became aware of each stage after the fact, not before, based on circumstances that made it overwhelmingly self-evident. I was building the plane as I was flying it, roughly speaking.

One last thing. I mentioned this in the beginning of the book, but it's worth repeating. *In sterquiliniis invenitur,* i.e., what you most want to find is where you least want to look. The idea is, when you look where you least want to, you revivify the ancestral father, archetypally speaking—you give him new life through your own.

When Simba becomes king of Pride Rock, he gives new life to his father, Mufasa, who lives on through his son.

When Harry Potter accepts his wizardry, he embodies the best of his perished parents.

Same goes for Bruce Wayne as he became the Caped Crusader we all love.

Can't forget about Moses, the dude was afraid to speak to a burning bush; but then went on to become not only the greatest orator Israel has ever known, but God the Father referred to him as His *friend.*

Said plainly, Simba, Harry, Bruce, and Moses went all-in on their gift; they looked where they least wanted to and achieved self-mastery in the process. When *you* look where you least want to, going all-in on your gift, an expansive and rapid transformation takes place—you become Batman.

Just kidding. You won't become Batman. You'll just

realize who you've been all along; and in doing so, you will redefine your Default.

You will change your story.

And when you change your story, you change your life.

SECTION I: THE CALL TO ADVENTURE

The moment when the hero feels compelled to embark on a new journey. This feeling could be the result of a message, a dream, or a calling from a mentor or guide.

A Quantum Leap

May 16, 2022

"Alright," the Managing Partner at the financial firm's office said, pushing my contract across the mahogany table. "Here's a list of targets to aim for in your first year, and if you just sign below—"

"Executive Council?" I said, tapping the bottom of the page. "What's that?"

He crossed his arms. "It's a special award for any agent who makes fifty thousand dollars or more in first year commissions," he said, pushing a hand through the air. "It's quite an accomplishment—especially for a first-year agent. Don't worry, it's something to shoot for. It's not a requirem—"

"What's the fastest it's been done in this office?" I asked.

He cocked his head like a dog might. "In this office?" He looked at my manager, John, and shrugged. "Twelve weeks, I think?"

I did it in half that time.

July 7, 2022

I was driving down I-96 on my way to Oconto, Wisconsin. I had a birthday party to attend—Kyle Galik's daughter, Alivia.

Yeah, *that* Kyle.

Since starting my career in finance, I reconnected with him and Bill.[24] Kyle even bought a life insurance policy. And now I was on my way to spend the weekend with them. I had my best friend back, and the only guy I felt comfortable calling me "son" since my dad died.

Life was good.

The drive was just over six hours. Plenty of time for a good podcast or two. With no traffic on the road, I grabbed my phone. I thumbed down YouTube. The algorithm brought me an episode of *London Real*—a video talk show where host, Brian Rose, introduces viewers to the most fascinating people on the planet. His guest on the episode, I found, fit the description: a business tycoon internationally known as *The Trillion Dollar Man,*[25] Mr. Dan S. Peña.

Mr. Peña was a well-dressed, vulgar-as-the-day-is-long old man who was passionate about one thing: helping people stop self-sabotage; mainly through the creation of generational wealth in as little as thirty-six months.

Tiffany had mentioned this *Trillion Dollar Man* to me before, showing me a clip here and there on Instagram. *Hmm.* I thought, then set my phone down, turning the volume knob on the dash to the right.

---

[24] One of the things most financial firms do to help kickstart a new agent's business is encouraging them to talk to their "warm market" i.e., friends and family. I just went into the contacts list on my phone and started calling people. Bill and Kyle were ecstatic to hear from me despite losing touch with them the past several years.

[25] Over the course of Mr. Peña's thirty years of financial coaching, his methodology—which I'll get into shortly—has helped more than one million people become millionaires; the product of one million and one million is one trillion, hence the moniker.

Rose dove right in, asking Mr. Peña how he accomplished such remarkable results with his mentees and devotees.

Mr. Peña was proud to elaborate. He spoke about his Quantum Leap Advantage (QLA) methodology, in which the sole premise is to buy a business with no money.

It's not a scam, I promise. QLA comes down to one thing: a *Motivated Seller*.

Once you find that needle-in-a-haystack, if he is truly a *Motivated Seller*—meaning he'll do anything to get out from underneath his business—the rest is just details.

What's the cash flow?

How are you going to structure the deal—seller financed or are you going to partner with a bank?

Is the deal enticing enough for lawyers and accountants to work on a *success fee* basis? Meaning, they don't get paid a dime until the day the deal closes?

Is the business owner going to stay on for a year or so to help with the transition?

Details.

But if you don't have a *Motivated Seller*, QLA will never work.

It just won't.

This was interesting to me, but not nearly as interesting as how, for a select few, he taught the methodology in-person at his *fifteenth century castle* in Forfar, Scotland for a weeklong QLA seminar.

Mr. Peña shared what a typical week at a seminar consisted of in addition to learning his wealth-building methodology firsthand.

Three-piece suits worn by the attendees.

Class begins at eight in the morning, ending at eleven or later at night.

Homework to be completed and emailed to him before breakfast the next morning.

Butlers waiting on you hand and foot; four course

meals.

Surrounded by luxury.

A stunning view of the sun rising over the golf course on which the castle was nestled.

The whole nine.

Then Mr. Peña shared his upbringing. The similarities between us were striking.

He believed in Santa Claus until he was eleven. So did I.

He cut his teeth selling insurance. I was having a good time selling it myself.

He was a marathoner-turned-powerlifter. I was a powerlifter-turned-sprinter.

His message was simple: follow your passion—something I had tried to do and failed miserably more than once.

"But most kids *don't* follow their passion." Mr. Peña said.

"And why is that?" Rose asked.

"Self-sabotaging activities." Mr. Peña shrugged. "It's their *Default*—and Default's a b****!" (Mr. Peña had a proclivity for choice language; language I'll spare you from).

Default? I thought, feeling my eyebrows knit together. *Huh.*

Out of the millions of devotees and thousands of castle seminar attendees, Rose asked Mr. Peña how many people he's mentored personally over his thirty years of teaching QLA.

"I only work with people I've trained in-person at the castle," Mr. Peña said. "I don't care how good your idea or business is, if I haven't trained you, I won't mentor you."

I had heard enough.

I knew then and there he and I were going to work together in some form or fashion.

I knew, though I didn't know how, I was going to get to

a QLA seminar at his castle.

I knew I needed to get in front of Mr. Peña. And when I did, I knew Mr. Peña was going to help me stop my self-sabotage once and for all—no matter the cost.

The Call to Adventure.

SECTION II: REFUSAL OF THE CALL

The moment when the hero balks at the Call to Adventure. He is stymied by fear, lack of resources, and feelings of inadequacy.

Next

July 11, 2022

There was a QLA seminar in October.

The cost to attend?

Just over $31K—excluding travel.

Tiffany and I were fans of Mr. Peña, just not at that price point.

Sure, I was off to a fast start with insurance, but I couldn't shell out more than half my commissions in one fell swoop. Let's be honest, you know me well enough by now to know that kind of stupidity wasn't beneath me.

So, what was the real reason why I was hesitant to pull the trigger?

On my way to work one morning, I was listening to Mr. Peña answer questions submitted to him through his website. One question was: "Has QLA ever worked for an *author?"*

"No," Mr. Peña said. "Next."

There goes that idea. I thought as I pulled into my parking spot.

Yeah, the cost of the seminar played a factor. But how in the hell was I going to make QLA work as an author when I was hardly a writer for God's sake?

As soon as I got to my office, my boss, John, was waiting for me. He told me the company was issuing a third quarter incentive: a $2.5K bonus to the agent who led their General Office with life insurance cases.

With the price tag of QLA being astronomical, the fact that Mr. Peña's methodology never worked for an author, and the firm's third quarter incentive being right up my alley, the idea of attending QLA and being mentored by Mr. Peña was all it was—an idea.

Refusal of the Call.

SECTION III: SUPERNATURAL AID

The hero encounters a guide, or mentor, who gives the hero the courage to embark on the journey.

The Billion Dollar Idea

October 6, 2022

I was kissing-distance from my office window. The Grand River was a cool band of blue running through downtown Grand Rapids under a faded-denim cloudless sky.

It was a pleasant combination.

Unfortunately, and I mean that technically, I had an unpleasant combination in my life insurance business.

Winning the third quarter incentive was good.

Clogging underwriting worse than a Calcutta sewer with more than twenty new clients was not good—most of the policies I'd written were close to their sixty-day deadlines.[26]

That meant two things:

- If the policy was not issued on or before sixty days after the application was submitted, my client(s) would lose their temporary coverage.
- My commission on the policy(s) would be reversed—I'd lose money.

---

[26] When a life insurance application is submitted, the proposed insured (i.e. the client) works in tandem with underwriting to see if they're insurable and what their risk rating will be. This process has a sixty-day deadline for the policy to be paid for and issued. I had written so many policies that quarter, underwriting was having difficulty keeping up.

You can surmise which of the two things had my attention.

I wrote an email to our Life Insurance Consultant in Ohio. The note read:

> *Are we the biggest and baddest mutual company on the planet? Because if we are, we ought to start acting like it; I've got nearly twenty clients who've been stuck in underwriting for almost sixty days now and they're getting antsy. If Amazon ever starts selling life insurance, we are screwed.*

If Amazon ever starts selling life insurance, I thought.

I was in John's office sixty seconds later.

"Nobody's doing that," he said, passing a hand down his face after hearing my Amazon life insurance idea. He stood up, hooking his thumbs in either belt loop as he gazed out the window. "That's a helluva idea—a billion-dollar idea."

John's reflection in the window suggested he was imagining what could be, or perhaps what could have been. He swung a look over his shoulder. "You remind me of me, y'know."

I cocked my head, thinking it was an odd thing to say.

"I used to be a runner—a runner in business. Your tenacity reminds me of me."

"Used to be?"

John shrugged. "I slowed down," he said. "Always wanted to be a writer. I've got three books at home I've never finished."

Before I could ask why, John pushed a hand through the air in a dismissive fashion. "We ought to step out; do our own thing," John said, placing both hands, knuckles down, on the cherry-colored desk between us. "Call it *J. Smith and Associates.* You can even be the CEO. I don't care."

"You're not serious."

"I just turned fifty-nine years old and I ain't got nothing to show for it," he bowed his head, then looked at me and said: "Yes I'm serious."

A Worthy Investment—Part One

October 7, 2022

With no progress being made on my clients' underwriting, not being awarded my bonus yet for winning the third quarter incentive, and another QLA seminar added for November, I was pissed off just enough to do something stupid.

I decided to pitch myself to someone I thought could help get me to QLA—the man who's always been there for me, no matter how much time has passed between us; and he's always believed in me.

"Hunter," Bill Galik said, answering the phone.

"Hey," I said. "Got something I want to run by you."

I explained the situation. I told him my Amazon insurance idea, paired with Mr. Peña's guidance, mentorship—which was no sure thing, by the way—and methodology would turn the financial industry upside down. Not to mention we'd make a fortune.

Bill's response?

"I would invest in Hunter Charneski."

The money was wired to Mr. Peña's assistant a couple hours later.

Tiffany and I were over-the-moon.

I was on my way to QLA.

Supernatural Aid.

SECTION IV: CROSSING THE FIRST THRESHOLD

The hero leaves behind the Ordinary World and crosses into the Extraordinary World, demonstrating a new ability, or power, he didn't know he had.

Put God First—Part One

October 12, 2022

With my seat secured for QLA in November, I resigned from the firm.

Yep. Just like that.

There I was, on track to be one of, if not the greatest, first-year agents in Michigan General Office history, and I quit over $2.5K—the incentive I had expected.

If that isn't self-sabotage, I don't know what is.

November 2, 2022

I wasn't an insurance free agent for long.

I signed with an insurance firm specializing in final expense policies.[27]

I picked up right where I left off at my old firm, Number One on the leaderboard after my first week. I liked their sales process, it was more my speed.

Buy a list of leads.

Make three hundred cold calls per day.

Close the prospects over-the-phone.

---

[27] Final expense, meaning smaller face values ($10-25K), in order to cover the costs of the burial and funeral to alleviate the financial burden of the insured's family after their death.

Turn a "no" into a "yes."

Buy or die. That was the game.

That *was* the game, until Mr. Jones picked up the phone.

"I need a universal life insurance policy," Mr. Jones said.

What I thought was going to be a one-call-close turned into a six-hour conversation with a complete stranger.

What on earth were you talking about? You're probably wondering.

Nothing on *earth.* Look up.

Mr. Jones gave me a masterclass on God that day. And I'm not convinced the dude wasn't God Himself. I mean, he sounded exactly like Morgan Freeman in *Bruce Almighty.* And maybe he was, because I told that guy everything. During our six-hour conversation, I told him all of my hopes, my dreams, all the good I wanted to do—

"Put God first," he said. "Or you will lose *everything.*"

Whoa.

Now God, like Mr. Jones and I, were complete strangers.

Sure, I believed in Him. But I never had gotten to know Him. There's a yawning chasm between believing in and befriending someone. So, after chatting with Mr. Jones that day, I tried putting God first. I picked up *His* phone, if you will, by reading the Bible first thing in the morning, every morning.

I never did sell Mr. Jones any life insurance.

Perhaps he didn't need any.

Perhaps I did.

Perhaps I was the one being sold—sold on *the* universal life insurance policy that is Jesus Christ—and it didn't cost me a dime. What a gift.

Who knows, maybe I was on the phone with God that day?

Tiffany thought I was, perhaps she was right.

The Seminar

November 16, 2022

THE TRILLION DOLLAR MAN was in all capital letters behind the stage where an empty chair idled.

Twenty-three attendees and myself awaited Mr. Peña's arrival on opening night.

I was in the front row. There was some chatter and whispering conversations amongst the group. I said nothing to no one. I wasn't there to make friends. I was there for one thing: to sell Mr. Peña on me.

Then silence blanketed the room.

Out of the corner of my right eye, a tall, well-dressed man rounded the edge of the stage.

It's him, I thought, swallowing hard as Mr. Peña walked on stage and found his chair. It's a weird feeling to be in the presence of someone whose net worth exceeds $600M.

Mr. Peña took a look at us, seemingly grimacing in disgust.

Here's one thing you have to understand about Mr. Peña: He's hard. He's the Bobby Knight of the personal development/wealth creation industry—if Bobby Knight was on steroids. Mr. Peña's target audience are primarily young to middle aged men[28]—Self-Sabotaging Men, at that.

---

[28] Not to say women aren't invited, or encouraged to attend QLA; of the twenty four attendees, three were female. No different than this book. I'm not saying women aren't invited or encouraged to read this

Men who, by and large, didn't have a strong and authoritative male role model, or father figure, during their most formative years. Men who are, consciously or not, seeking the tough love they never got from someone they respect and admire.

And make no mistake, these men, myself included, respected and admired Mr. Peña. Deep down we knew he was trying his best to get us to stop sabotaging ourselves. He, like Bobby Knight, had his own unique way of doing so—and that's what draws his audience to him. But as vulgar and insulting as Mr. Peña can be, it was obvious how passionate he was about helping us. He's hard, but not hard-hearted. He is one of the most genuinely caring men I have ever met, despite his speech being riddled with F-bombs.

"You're all here because the program works," Mr. Peña said, nodding to himself affirmingly. "This week is going to be a transformative week. Let's begin…."

November 19, 2022

QLA was as advertised.

Class from 8AM till 11PM, if not later.

World-class food and service all day long by Mr. Peña's personal butler, Duncan, and his staff.

And of course, learning Mr. Peña's methodology on how to create generational wealth.

On Day Four however, it was clear my Amazon insurance idea was not the path I was going to take.

"If you stick to what you know, you're gonna fail!"[29]

---

book, women self-sabotage too. But they're not my target audience. Same goes for QLA.

[29] A soberingly similar corollary to what we've been discussing thus

Mr. Peña said, leering at us with wolf-like eyes. "Pick an industry you know nothing about and you've got a chance. HealthCare is hot and it's gonna *stay hot* till kingdom come!"

Fair enough.

HealthCare it was.

Where I was going to begin, or what I was going to do, I hadn't the slightest idea. My only experience with HealthCare, as Mr. Peña lauded about it, was my dad's slow death in hospice.

After lunch, Mr. Peña began the second half of Day Four by discussing how to build one's board of directors, or what he calls: *The Dream Team.*

The Dream Team consists of a chairman, founding director (the QLA attendee), chief executive officer, chief financial officer, an accountant, a lawyer, and three industry experts.

The most important seat on The Dream Team was Chairman. The Chairman typically has the most experience and, more importantly, he's the one who genuinely believes in the Founding Director. Having the backing of the chairman blocks the other board members from balking at the Founding Director's direction.

"Don't ask me to be your chairman!" Mr. Peña said. He took a deep breath and continued: "If you came all this way just to ask me to be your chairman, you wasted your money."

In Mr. Peña's thirty years of teaching QLA, he has chaired only a small number of Dream Teams for a select few individuals—all of which he's helped make hundreds of millions, if not *billions,* of dollars.

His success rate on Dream Teams he's chaired is one hundred percent.

"Don't ask me to be your chairman, because I'll say

---

far. Sticking to what you know leads to self-sabotage.

'no.' I'm the Goldman Sachs of chairmen. Just ask the kids I've worked with. The ones who've been super successful have said—" Mr. Peña straightened his tie. "'We listened to Mr. Peña's advice like it was the *Word of God.'* But super success isn't for everyone." He sighed. "And besides, I'm stepping out of the chairman business."

"Now, my daughter, Kelly, unlike you…she didn't understand what 'no' meant when she was little," he said, straightening his tie. "Probably why [she] leads the nation in sales at her company every single year!"

We said nothing.

Mr. Peña craned his neck back, looking up at the ceiling as if he was reliving memories in his mind's eye. "To her, 'no' meant 'yes'." he said, chuckling. "When I told her 'No, Kelly,' she learned at a very young age to ask, 'I know Daddy, but what would I have to do to turn that 'no' into a 'yes?''"

Mr. Peña snickered, then gestured his hand through the air like a knife through warm butter, glaring at us. "Anyways, I'm stepping out of the chairman business, so don't ask me. I'll be eighty in three years and then I'm going to run for parliament."

Then he scooted to the edge of his seat, passed a hand down his black pinstripe three-piece suit, watched us and said: "Now, since some of you are as thick as two short planks, I'll say it once more: don't ask me to be your chairman. Understand? *Verstehen?*"[30]

Everyone nodded.

Everyone except me.

---

[30] "Understand?" in German, as there were more than a handful of attendees from Germany. Mr. Peña was being facetious.

The Way—Part Five

November 21, 2022

Graduation Night at Guthrie Castle.

The men wore kilts. The women wore cocktail dresses. The festivities began with a bagpipe demonstration that still echoes in some deep valley of my head followed by certificates and pictures with Mr. Peña.[31]

Image 4: Graduation Night with Mr. Peña at Guthrie Castle, source: Hunter M. Charneski

[31] In my left hand is a bottle of Mr. Peña's whiskey—not to be opened until you complete your first deal.

After dinner in Guthrie Castle's private dining room, all attendees gathered in the drawing room.

There were cameras everywhere.

The stage was set for Mr. Peña's YouTube channel's series: *Stories of the Trillion Dollar Man.*

Mr. Peña lived up to it, sharing story after story with us, sipping on a White Russian as he did. Something warm brewed inside me. It waxed hotter as the minutes passed. It wanted to get out. I had to listen to it. When Mr. Peña finished his drink, he made an all-encompassing gesture with his hand, giving the floor to whoever had something to say.

Mr. Peña shared his stories.

Now I'd share mine.

I waved Duncan, the butler, over. He handed me the mic.

"At the beginning of the week," I said, approaching the middle of the drawing room. "You said it would be a transformative week."

"Yes, sir," Mr. Peña said, nodding.

"I'm sure we can all agree it has surely been that," I said. "The other piece I've gleaned from you this week, Mr. Peña, is *clarity.*" I paused. "On September fifth, two thousand five, my dad died. I was fourteen years old."

I recalled the time when my mom asked him whether he wanted me there when he died.

"Fast forward two weeks," I said. "The night he died, the hospice nurse said, 'I'll be surprised if he makes it past midnight.' Me being naive back then," I shrugged. "Not much has changed."

Mr. Peña appreciated the self-deprecation, chortling in his chair.

"I kissed him on the forehead and said, 'I'll see you tomorrow, dad.' And I went home." I sighed. "Half-an-hour later, my phone rang. 'Hunter, your dad is gone.'"

The attendees offered a collective moan.

"For seventeen years, I have been wondering why my

dad didn't want me to be there when he died. And it was only during this week, Mr. Peña, that I found that reason out. And it hit me like an effing ton of bricks." I said, clenching my fist in front of me. "It was because my dad didn't want his son to see him die with regrets."

I paused, staring at Mr. Peña. He stared right back at me.

"Do you have any idea how much that means to me?"

Mr. Peña placed a hand over *where his heart should have been,* as he'd say, and said: "I do know, yeah."[32]

I nodded. "And so that gives me immense clarity moving forward because I know how my story will end. I will be damned if my son sees me die with regrets. And Mr. Peña, had I not come here, I can say beyond a shadow-of-a-doubt I would not know that answer. Thank you so much."

I approached Mr. Peña, offering my hand.

"You're very welcome," Mr. Peña said, accepting my handshake then leading the round of applause.

That night, though I didn't know it yet, was the first display of what was yet to come; of a gift I didn't know I had—my ability to speak extemporaneously.

Crossing the First Threshold.

---

[32] In hindsight, I think he really did know, which makes this story all the more powerful, which you'll see near the end.

SECTION V: BELLY OF THE WHALE

The hero reaches the point of no return. He must now see the journey through its completion.

The Chairman

November 22, 2022

One of the perks of attending the QLA seminar is a one-on-one, thirty-minute meeting with Mr. Peña—what he calls *private time.* As fate would have it, my private time with Mr. Peña just happened to be on the last day. This was my chance, my one and only chance to pitch myself to Mr. Peña.

I wasn't going to get this opportunity again.

I rehearsed my pitch all morning.

Outside my guest cottage before sunrise.

In the pavilion after breakfast.

I wrote notes in blue ink on my palms in case I forgot something.

I even recited the affirmation: "I want to have Mr. Peña as my chairman. I am happily and easily having Mr. Peña as my chairman." over and over again on a walk through his estate until I cried—I'm serious. The prospect of being mentored by The Trillion Dollar Man brought tears to my eyes.

"Hunter," Mr. Peña's assistant, Kim, poked her head in the castle's trophy room where I was waiting, pushing her glasses up the blade of her nose, then nodding. "Mr. Peña will see you now."

There were frogs everywhere.

Yes, frogs.

Frogs adorned Mr. Peña's office.

Frog paperweights.

Frog ornaments hanging from the ceiling.

A pair of frog cufflinks.

Hell, even Smoochy, the frog Beanie Baby, was sitting on the corner of his desk.

Think of the movie *The Rite* with Anthony Hopkins. That's the kind of *frogage* I'm talking about.

All of which were more than fitting. One of Mr. Peña's most notorious *Peñaisms* is: "To be successful, you've got to kiss a lot of frogs."

"How can I help you?" Mr. Peña said, sitting with his right leg crossed over his left, his eyes fixed on my file. My file contained a shortlist of questions I had written and sent to Kim two weeks before arriving at the castle; a shortlist of questions for this very moment.

I forgot every question I wrote except one, probably because that was the only question that mattered to me. The question was: *Has the QLA Methodology worked in the Arts? Specifically, writers?*

Then I committed perhaps the greatest act of self-sabotage in front of the guy who was *in the business* of stopping self-sabotage.

"With all due respect, Mr. Peña," I said, shaking my head and unbuttoning my suit jacket as I sat down. "You can wipe your ass with that because that's about all it's worth."

Mr. Peña shrugged, then nodded, setting my file beside him. He wrung his hands together, and nodded, cuing me to begin.

Sweat ran down my spine like warm oil.

I pushed myself to a stand, buttoned my suit jacket and said: "First of all, I want to begin by saying I meant what I said last night."

Mr. Peña nodded and smiled.

So far so good, I thought.

That bit of throat-clearing helped ease me into my pitch. I touched on all our similarities. From believing in Santa till we were eleven to powerlifting and everything in between. Then came the big ask: "If you really want to help me, Mr. Peña, the best way you can do so is by being my chairman."

"No, no," Mr. Peña said, waving his hands. He shook his head and said: "I appreciate your offer but I'm stepping out of the chairman business."[33]

"I understand Mr. Peña," I said, then bent over and looked the Trillion Dollar Man in the eyes. "But lemme ask you, what would I have to do to turn that 'no' into a 'yes?'"

Belly of the Whale.

---

[33] At that point in his career, "chairman business" would have been mostly me using his name and track record to lure Dream Team members. From there, he would get involved only at in-person board meetings—maybe one or two a year—when we would be moving forward with acquiring companies.

SECTION VI: ROAD OF TRIALS

The hero's skills, courage, and character is put to the test. These events can be physical, such as battles or competitions, or psychological, such as facing inner demons or overcoming personal weaknesses.

The Golden Calf—Part One

Mr. Peña agreed to be my chairman on two conditions:

- He wanted to know how many home health care and assisted living facilities were in a 500-mile radius of Grand Rapids, Michigan.
- It had to be a big number.

The number was just over 8,000. After letting him know, he sent an email in all red, capitalized letters:

MORE THAN ENUF 2 GIT STARTED!

FIND 60-DAY DEADLINE ATTACHED! TO UR QL IN LIFE & BIZ!

- DAN

The outline for getting my first deal done was as follows:

- Chairman and Completed Board: 10 Days
- Outside Accountant/Lawyer: 10 Days...20 Total
- Pre-Interviewing Multiple Banks for Lending Parameters: 5 Days...25 Total
- Screening Multiple Motivated Seller Deals: 10 Days...35 Total
- LOI (Letters of Intent): 10 Days...45 Total
- Close Deal: 15 Days...60 Total

And just like that, I was in business with Mr. Peña.

Call it an overstatement, but it's true. It was easier for me to pitch Bill Galik to invest $30K in me, fly to Scotland for a weeklong seminar, and then convince *The Trillion Dollar Man* to be my chairman than to stop sabotaging my God-given gift of writing.

Change Your Story—Part One

November 28, 2022

In order to be successful with QLA, you have to be an extremely effective communicator. From pitching potential Dream Team members to convincing law firms and accounting firms to work on a success fee basis and everything else that comes with getting the first deal done, if you couldn't win with words, then you were in trouble.

Mr. Peña told me to join Toastmasters, Rotary Club, and Kiwanis. Clinging to every word he said as if it were the gospel, I happily obliged him. I became a regular visitor every Thursday at Grand Rapids Rotary Club. I became President of the closest Kiwanis Club. As for Toastmasters, there was a local club—the smallest in the entire district—just a few minutes from where I lived.

I was at my first Toastmasters meeting the Monday after I got home from Scotland. I'll admit, I thought I was already a decent public speaker. But I wanted to be better, more polished, and able to tell compelling stories.

Little did I know, that little Toastmasters club would help me change *my* story.

In sterquiliniis invenitur.

The Golden Calf—Part Two

December 5, 2022

Toastmasters was working.

Eleven days after leaving the castle, I had my Dream Team in place. Alongside the *Goldman Sachs of Chairmen,* Mr. Peña sat:

- The former CEO of Mercy Health, (now Trinity Health).
- The former CFO for Ford Motor Company's $2B North American Engine Manufacturing division, and then serving in the same role at seven healthcare companies since 2012.
- The former President and COO of Preferred HealthCare.
- A former partner from Big Four accounting firm, Ernst & Young.
- One of our industry experts served as former vice president Al Gore's on-call family doctor in addition to being our in-house lawyer, the other a leading research and technology developer at Wayne State University.

My Dream Team had more than 150 years of collective experience and a combined track record of over $50B dollars in acquisitions in the HealthCare industry. Together, we were Luminary HealthCare, and I was on track to meeting

Mr. Peña's sixty-day deadline.

Speaking of track, I was at the track that morning. The plan was to do a quick tune-up workout before my first indoor meet of the year—just four days from then.

That was the plan, at least.

After I was done warming up, there was a hardness in my left calf. It felt like someone lodged a lacrosse ball in it. It was unsettling, but I was no stranger to that sort of thing, given my size and injury history. I just chalked it up to the typical aches and pains of being an athlete.

But when I put my spikes on, I felt something else. I can hardly describe it, like a black column of dread filling one vertebrae at a time. It's paradoxical to say, but it wasn't just a feeling: It was loud but I couldn't hear it—a voice without sound. It was strong, too, like gravity. *That* was unsettling; whatever was going on with my calf couldn't hold a candle to that feeling.

It was as if I wasn't supposed to sprint that day.

I shook it off, then parroted one of Mr. Peña's *Peñaisms:* "Do something every day that scares you."

So, I approached the start line.

The black column was touching my cervical spine now.

I had a deep sense of dread.

I knew it wasn't going to end well.

Naturally, I did it anyway.

I took a staggered stance, left leg forward and right leg back. I inhaled deeply, then rolled over my front knee, pushing myself away from the line, putting on speed.

At thirty meters, everything felt as it should.

I was smooth.

I was relaxed.

I was upright.

I was *fast.*

Then came sixty meters.

POP! went my left calf.

I cartwheeled my arms, decelerating as gingerly as I

could.

I limped back to the bench and laughed. It was kind of a laugh but not really a laugh at all. More like some sick giggle from the twisted pleasure of self-inflicted pain I took part in.

I knew I was going to get hurt and I ran anyway.

I knew that doing so would keep me from competing four days later.

I knew I should have listened to whatever that voice-like feeling was, but I listened to Mr. Peña's instead.

My Golden Calf.

Change Your Story—Part Two

December 19, 2022

Twenty-five days had passed since returning home from QLA, and I was five days behind schedule to meet Mr. Peña's sixty-day deadline.

Getting a law firm to work on a success fee basis was easier than selling mud to a pig.

An accounting firm? That was another story—and I mean that technically.

I called more than one hundred firms all across the country. None were interested in working on a success fee basis. I had Zoom calls with close to fifty others. As soon as they found out they'd be working for free indefinitely, the call was over.

That morning, I rehearsed a speech in my office seventeen times[34] before pounding the pavement in downtown Grand Rapids—on a strained calf, mind you—pitching close to a dozen firms in-person the rest of the day.

All were met with polite declinations.

At a quarter till five, I had one last pitch to make. It was to Deloitte—the largest accounting firm in the world.

"We typically don't work on a success fee basis." The

---

[34] Why seventeen? Couldn't tell you. It sounded like a good number to end on.

office's Managing Partner said. "We can run it up the chain of command and get back to you."

Running it up the chain of command would take time.

Time isn't something I had.

"This is Dan Peña we're talking about!" I said, pounding my fist on the table like a judge's gavel. "And I'm the guy who *brought the billionaire* out of retirement. You think he'd get involved with me if he didn't think I was gonna be a success?"

The only thing the Managing Partner thought I'd be successful in was finding my way out of the building. He thanked me for the time, yammering on about how he needed to get some last-minute Christmas shopping done as he escorted me to the elevators.

Speaking of Christmas, I had a nice little stocking stuffer waiting for me when I got back to my car.

"Nice." I said, plucking the parking ticket from underneath my windshield wiper. I climbed in the car, slammed the door shut and smacked the steering wheel. That was the first moment I began to doubt what I was doing. Tiffany was counting on me to get a deal done—because we needed money like we needed air. Instead of coming home to share the good news of partnering with an accounting firm, all I had to show for a long day's work was a fine from the city of Grand Rapids.

A calendar notification pinged on my phone. It was a reminder that I had a Toastmasters meeting in fifteen minutes. And thank God for that. Becoming a better public speaker seemed to be the only thing I was successful at since returning home from QLA.

I wasn't going to stop now.

Starving—Part One

January 8, 2023

I finally found an accounting firm willing to partner with us on a success fee basis—a smaller, regional firm out of Green Bay, Wisconsin, my hometown coincidentally enough. From there, I interviewed a handful of banks in the area, all of which were more than willing to partner with us in financing if the deal was right. And with just thirteen days left to meet Mr. Peña's deadline, I was almost three weeks behind schedule. I was confident I could make up for the lost time. All I had to do now was what separated me from my peers when it came to selling life insurance—cold calling.

Less than two hundred dials later, I found a *Motivated Seller*. He owned a few adult foster care facilities in Grand Rapids, and a handful of others scattered throughout Michigan. After obtaining his financials and tax returns, my CFO found out why he was so motivated—his business was over $1M in debt.

Despite that rather large blemish, and all the banks I'd spoken to saying that much debt wasn't a deal they wished to finance—they didn't share the same sentiment as Bill Galik when it came to investing in me—there was still a way we could get this deal done. My CFO and Dream Team crafted a Letter of Intent for a 100% seller-financed deal.

We've discussed the importance of finding that one *Motivated Seller*. The reason why the *Motivated Seller* is so important for Mr. Peña's QLA methodology is because that's how you'll be able to buy a business with no money. Enter the 100% seller-financed deal. Here's how it works, roughly speaking. The cash flow generated from the business is the money that's paid to the business owner, typically over five years in monthly installments with a larger payout at the end of the agreement. Ideally, payments wouldn't begin until one year after the deal is closed, so the business owner can help with the transition in power and operations. Essentially, you're buying the business from the business owner with his own money. *Who in their right mind would do that?* You're probably wondering. Not just anyone, that's for sure. But a *Motivated Seller* would. He's owned the business his entire life. Now it owns him. He can't break free from it. Sure, the business prints money, but it's death by a thousand (paper) cuts. He's got staffing issues. He's working all day and night. He hasn't taken a vacation in fifteen years. He's sick and tired. He's desperate to sell. He will do anything to get out from underneath it—including a 100% seller-financed deal.

January 13, 2023

The business owner and I got brunch that morning. I presented him with the Letter of Intent for a 100% seller-financed deal. He signed it.

"I knew you would do it," Tiffany said to me on the phone when I told her.

My jubilation was short-lived, however. The accounting firm reneged on their willingness to work with us on a success fee basis.

Screw it. I thought.

I had eight days left to meet Mr. Peña's deadline. Their due diligence would have taken time. And I didn't have any to spare. I was prepared to move forward with the deal without them.[35]

I didn't care what it took.

We needed money.

I was starving to get that deal done.

January 15, 2023

Forty-eight hours after signing the Letter of Intent, the business owner decided he wasn't willing to move forward with the deal unless we came with the cash to get him out of debt. We were so close.

Six days out from Mr. Peña's sixty-day deadline, the deal officially died.

I sent Mr. Peña an email notifying him the deal had fallen through. Despite that, I assured him we would still meet the sixty-day deadline. How? Your guess is as good as mine.

His response:

SCREW YOUR SIXTY DAYS! MAN UP!

Okay then. If Mr. Peña didn't care about his own deadline, why should I?

Speaking of manning up, I had gotten my calf healthy enough to sprint. And there was a meet coming up that weekend—January 21, the sixty-day deadline, oddly enough—and I was ready to run. I was starving for it.

---

[35] No due diligence is a special kind of stupid. Due diligence ensures the business is actually making what its owner claims it's making, which is why you want accountants. Due diligence is the accountants' job.

Starving—Part Two

January 21, 2023

"On your marks…" the starter said into the megaphone.

I took three deep breaths, stepped over my starting blocks, and crowded the start line.

I made exactly three arm swings.

Another deep breath.

I reached down, touched my toes.

I walked my hands six inches or so ahead of the start line.

I pressed my palms on the royal blue track.

I pushed my left foot into the front block. My right foot into the back block.

With my feet set, I walked my hands back. Left hand, then right. I made my hands into teepee-shapes behind the start line. I swayed side-to-side twice, letting my head loll like a spineless doll. I fixed my gaze on the worn and scabby white paint of the start line.

One last deep breath.

I let it out slowly through pursed lips, warm and hissing as I waited for—

"Set!"

Inhaling through my nose, expanding my ribs, feeling my abs brace themselves. I raised my hips.

POW!

I leapt out of the blocks.

By the time I had my first conscious thought—near the two-hundred-meter mark—I was in the lead.

Then the flood came.

The *flood* is not a good thing. There's no getting away from it no matter how good of shape you're in. It is a wave of acidosis as my body shifted from the alactic energy system (reserved for short, explosive bouts) to lactic, or glycolytic (energy system used for activities ranging roughly between thirty and ninety seconds).

My posture stiffened, pulling me back from my slight forward lean till I was shaped like the parentheses above the nine on a keyboard. At two hundred fifty meters, my shoulders went from loose and free to taught and restrained. I felt my glutes swell as if I were slowly morphing into a male representation of Jennifer Lopez.

By three hundred meters, the swelling spread like cancer to my quads. My legs went from powerful pistons to wobbly stacks of pencil erasers. Then came the final turn. My ankles felt like stumps. My body was a cement-filled vase.

I loped through the finish line, finishing second-to-last.

Despite the terrible finish, my time was 57.59—within one second of my all-time personal record of 56.63. Having just turned thirty-two years old, weighing two hundred thirty pounds, and not being nearly in the kind of shape I could have been had it not been for the calf strain a month prior, I was elated.

"Okay then," I said, blowing a kiss to Tiffany looking on in the stands as I walked back to my duffel bag. "It's gonna be a good year."

A couple hours later is when it happened.

Typically after a meet, Tiff and I would either go out to dinner or make something extravagant at home. That night we went with the latter.

Filet mignon was on the menu.

Mini bagels, a loaf of bread, two sleeves of Oreos, and an entire jar of peanut butter weren't.

I didn't care.

I didn't stop eating.

I *couldn't* stop eating.

Binge-eating had been a problem for several months at that point. I'd overeat as often as once per week and as infrequently as once per month. Binge-eating is a form of self-sabotage in general. But it's especially sabotaging for an already oversized sprinter, where every extra pound of bodyweight is working against me as I run down the track.

There I was, a few hours removed from opening my season within one second of my personal record in the 400-meter dash, and I binged myself all the way back to the starting line.

Behind the starting line, more like it.

Let's not be melodramatic. One binge wouldn't negate all the training and preparation I had done up to that point. One day doesn't make you and one day doesn't break you.

That isn't the point.

The point is I was starving; starving for something more than food.

No matter how much I ate, I wasn't satisfied. Christ wasn't kidding when He said: "Man shall not live on bread alone."

Which begs the question, what was I starving for?

Go All-In—Part One

Go All-In was the central concept of my personal development group, *Artistic Warrior.*

I still have a box of t-shirts with the phrase on the back to prove it.

The concept is simple, but simple doesn't mean easy. You can know what *Go All-In* means without knowing what it takes.

Case in point: as I'm writing this, it is May 2, 2024.

I don't know how many drafts I've written. If I had to guess, I'd say somewhere between fifteen and twenty—just because Stephen King said in *On Writing* all it takes is three drafts doesn't mean that's the case for everyone. My literary agent has pitched the book twice—once late last year under a different working title and again just a few weeks ago after changing the working title and revamping the book proposal. There's been some interest in the book, which is encouraging, but you're either pregnant or you're not. Without a book deal, the book won't be born. To give you some perspective, I signed with my agent on June 16, 2023. She and I have been working on getting a book deal done for almost a year now. Who knows how long it will take till I actually see the bloody thing on the shelves at Barnes & Noble. It could be another year or two, easy.

So yeah, to *Go All-In* isn't easy, especially when the tree you planted doesn't seem to be growing; much less, producing any fruit.

This is primetime for Default. That's certainly been the case for me, at least. When you *Go All-In* on your gift, but don't see results, it can be easier (and faster) to bring other things to life. Things others might see as noteworthy or as tremendous accomplishments.

Things like becoming a freak-of-nature athlete.

Resurrecting not one, but two businesses.

Can't forget shadow careers.

In other words, after planting the seed that will one day be a mighty oak tree able to stand the test of time, you grow impatient.

You plant a weed beside it.

The weed springs up quickly.

Seeing the growth happen almost in real time, the distraction-of-a-shadow-careering-Golden-Calf chokes your gift, stifling its growth and maturation. Killing it, even.

Perhaps that's what it means to "weed out" those who can't hack it—those who don't know what it means to *Go All-In* but don't know what it takes.

As I touched on in Part One, *Go All-In* doesn't necessarily mean abdicating any and all responsibility in lieu of your gift. That's what former Navy SEAL Jocko Willink would call a *classic overcorrection.* However, there may be critical moments where going all-in means doing nothing but writing your book, composing your symphony, or building your business. In my experience, those moments are exactly that—moments. But not always, as you'll read in Part Three.

Most of the time, going all-in on your gift may look like squeezing in fifteen precious minutes in a day while the rest of the day is devoted to a job that's slowly getting your family out of debt. Other times, going all-in may look like getting up at five in the morning so you can have an hour of unadulterated time to write your novel, sit at your easel, or turn that ball of clay into a flower pot.

I won't lie. There may be sometimes where you might not have *any* time to spend on your gift—you might go a day or two, or even a week, without working on it.

Don't stress about it.

Default loves it when you stress about it.

If you go a few days without working on your gift, here's a nice reframe I use: it's just like training. Some of my best workouts have come after a substantial amount of time off, typically three-to-seven days.

Why?

Because I'm rested. I'm itching to get back to it.

The same applies to time away from your gift.

If it's been a while since I've written, when I get back to it, I'm like a sprinter blasting out of the starting blocks. One thousand words in an hour ooze out of me, easily. What's more, there's content all around you that you can take back and apply to your gift.

Take my job for example. At Subway, there are stories to be told daily through interactions with my customers and staff. There are concepts abound I take directly from the job and can apply to my writing in order to illustrate a point clearly through metaphors or analogies. Like training, time off from your gift can be the best thing for it.

Go All-In is a simple concept, but simple doesn't mean easy.

Go All-In—Part Two

January 22, 2023

The next morning my stomach was distended, bloated with sugar and sodium from the epic binge just hours before then. I lay in bed wearing a hooded sweatshirt and sweatpants. The extra layer of clothes gave me a sense of feeling “hidden” from the extra four or five pounds I carried that morning.

I couldn’t hide from the shame and disgust, though.

Those emotions ate away at me.

“Enough of this, man,” I said, then did my best walrus impression, shimmying out of bed and making for my office.

Never again, I thought, rifling through my desk drawer for a dry erase marker. *This is the last effing time.* I thumbed the cap off the marker and wrote on my blackboard:

Image 5: The blackboard in my office, source: Hunter M. Charneski

The best prompt for writing is a provocative question.

It's been that way forever, and it'll be that way till Kingdom come.

The more the question pisses the writer off, the better.

Going off that presumption, what I wrote on my blackboard was the trillion-dollar question—and it pissed me off, royally.

I was at the point where I could do nothing else but rely on what I knew how to do best. Writing, combined with the intention to answer the question on my blackboard, was my only hope. I had starved myself of my gift for so long that my body, my soul, my mind, overthrew me in coup-like fashion, gorging in as much sustenance as possible.

I was subconsciously looking for what was truly nourishing for me.

I was starving for writing—the gift I knew I had since that day in Mrs. Schmitz's class—and no amount of bread, or food, would satisfy that hunger.

So, I started writing.

I had to solve my own problem.

I had to scratch my own itch.

I had to go off the script.

I went all-in on writing—the kind of writing I should have been doing all along, that is.

In hindsight, part of me thinks the race the day before was the deal that needed to get done—I met Mr. Peña's deadline in some weird way. Had it not been for that race, I may never have gotten on track to writing, or much less, finishing, this book.

Change Your Story—Part Three

January 23, 2023

Until this point, every speech I had given at Toastmasters was rehearsed, lasting seven-to-eight minutes. This night would send me on a different trajectory. Our club president made us aware of the *Table Topics* Area Championship happening a few weeks from then. Wanting our club to be represented, we had an impromptu club championship then and there.

As I touched on briefly in a footnote in the introduction, Table Topics is an extemporaneous spinoff of Toastmasters' public speaking format. Here's how it works: the speaker does not prepare, or rehearse a speech. Instead, he is asked a completely random question—in most cases, by the contest chair—and has roughly ten seconds to conjure up an answer. His answer must be at least sixty seconds long, but no longer than two-and-a-half minutes.

Speaking of answering questions, the question on my blackboard was top-of-mind. Would it be found through something as silly as Table Topics? Hell if I knew. But I wasn't about to leave that stone unturned. So, I volunteered to compete in our club championship that night—and I won, punching my ticket to the Area Championship in mid-February.

Writing and—now extemporaneous—speaking, though I was too close to the situation to see what was happening, helped me turn the corner.

I had made it out of the Road of Trials.

SECTION VII: MEETING WITH THE GODDESS

The hero meets with the other half of his internal being, represented by a powerful female, or heroine. In this stage, the hero experiences the power of unconditional love.

What Every Story Needs

February 3, 2023

Steven Pressfield said: "Every story needs to get to: 'I love you.'"

This story is no different.

Before meeting Tiffany, I had serious relationships with four other women. They were all great, more than I deserved. But Tiffany, lemme tell you. God knew what He was doing when He made her. The other women I dated eventually left me—and I don't blame them. Not one bit. Tiffany was the only one who never gave up on me.

Why? You might be wondering.

In her own words: "I saw your heart. I can't wait till you see how incredible you really are."

Wow.

Still in the throes of QLA, and desperately trying to answer the question on my blackboard through speaking and writing, it was Tiffany's idea to get married in a courthouse.

"Why not?" She said.

I mean, we *were* engaged. That wasn't exactly a Kodak moment, by the way. I had a diamond my mom gave me from her marriage with Andy. It was calling out to be worn—a gift waiting to be given, to be seen, to be appreciated—as any beautiful piece of art would. I decided to ask her to marry me a few months prior in our kitchen.

Hot stuff, I know.

Anyway, I took her up on her offer. We didn't need some extravagant wedding with cakes and disc jockeys and parties. We just wanted to get married, so we did.

Tiffany had watched me self-sabotage over and over again for the four-and-a-half years she knew me. She watched me fail with getting our first deal done with QLA. But instead of giving up on me, she married me, saying "I do."

Every story needs to get to "I love you."

Every story needs a Meeting with the Goddess.

SECTION VIII: TEMPTATION

The stage of the hero's journey in which the hero is distracted from his quest. The Temptation is most typically represented in the form of a desire, idol, or in this case, a Golden Calf.

Run *Your* Race—Part One

February 17, 2023

Last indoor meet of the season.

The first half of the 400-meter dash came and went before I had my first thought.

By 250 meters, I was nipping at the heels of this kid from a small division three school in Michigan, Hope College.

He was in first place. I was in second. I can still see my fingers grazing his flapping orange and blue jersey.

I was in a groove. My pace was perfect.

Until the final turn.

We were shoulder-to-shoulder at the home stretch. The crowd thundered. When I heard it, the exuberance-of-the-moment got the best of me.

I self-sabotaged, making a crucial mistake.

Near the end of the 400-meter dash, the *kick* happens. The *kick* means to sell out, fundamentally—whatever energy the runner has left, he gives 'er. The exact time and place to *kick* is unique to each runner. There's no standardized section, or zone, on the track that's indicative of where the *kick* should occur. The *kick* is incredibly nuanced to say the least. It requires incredible discipline. Each runner is racing against several others. Sometimes they're so close you can hear their breath and smell their body odor; but you can't focus on them, as paradoxical as it might sound. It's the race within the race—*your* race—you need to run if you're going to give yourself the best chance to win.

When you run *your* race, you won't make the crucial mistake I did by kicking too early and running out of steam before the finish line.

Despite that gaff, I did set a new personal record that day—clocking a time of 56.63 seconds.

But instead of winning, I came in third.

I was racing that kid from Hope College instead of running *my* race.

No matter your pursuit or passion; career or calling; goal or gift, run *your* race.

When you run *your* race, there's no competition.

Run *Your* Race—Part Two

"C'mon man. This is God-given. The only thing I gotta do is show up." — Derek Luke as Boobie Miles in the movie, *Friday Night Lights*

Running *your* race is a duality.

Run *Your* Race—Part One highlighted the importance of proper pacing and, more importantly, competing against yourself.

Here, it's about running the *right* race—the race you're meant to run.

Take me for example. I am not a distance runner. I could be, but I've trained hard and long enough since retiring from powerlifting to know that anything beyond the 400-meter dash isn't my race.

This concept isn't limited to track, or sports in general.

If your jam is journalism but you keep trying your hand at a novel, is it any wonder why you never finish?

If you're an opera singer but are conducting interviews in an attempt to be the next Oprah, that's a losing game.

If you're trying to get into fine-dining instead of doubling-down on the dishing out the meanest chili dogs this side of the Mississippi, help me understand why? Does it have something to do with the former being a Golden Calf—your Default of wanting more success? How's that program working out for you?

Your race is in franchises, not start-ups.

Your race is being an impressionist (like Claude Monet), not a cubist (like Pablo Picasso).

Your race is on stage at your local church, not the rat race in Hollywood.

Here's the cool thing about running *your* race. God has a way of making it obvious you're on the right track.

Because when you run *your* race, there's no competition.

February 18, 2023

The Toastmasters Table Topics Area Championship was the day after my last indoor meet. I took first place, winning by—you'll love this—*default.* The other gentleman who was representing our area was on vacation that day.

My first-place finish punched my ticket to the Division Championship in late March. All I had to do was show up.

Some might scoff at that. And fair enough. But as I said before: I think God likes to make it obvious when we're on the right track. Has He ever made it obvious to you? It's pretty cool when He does that, isn't it?

That's what happens when you run *your* race, and obviously, I was running mine.

When you run *your* race, there's no competition.

The Golden Calf—Part Three

February 23, 2023

I was writing in the morning, practicing a speech of some kind in the evening. Each speech was essentially another stab at answering the question on my blackboard: *Why do we sabotage ourselves?*

The week after winning the Table Topics Area Championship, I was introduced as a new member of the Grand Rapids Rotary Club—a club consisting of one hundred entrepreneurs and businesspeople. The club president invited me to come on stage and say a few words after being formally introduced.

Naturally, I told a story. I recalled that day in Mrs. Schmitz's class. To conclude, I said I wanted to help kids go all-in on the gift they know they have, but don't feel worthy enough to pursue because of life's adversities.

As soon as I stepped off the stage, a member of the club's leadership and head of the club's youth mentorship program approached me. "You're an incredible storyteller," she said. "Would you be interested in speaking to a group of high school students in mid-March?"

"Absolutely," I said.

March 2, 2023

Every first Thursday of the month, the Grand Rapids Rotary Club has a social hour at one of its member's businesses. Wanting to see if I could find another chance to speak, I went.

I met a guy there who worked at Mel Trotter Ministries—a homeless shelter in downtown Grand Rapids. His role there was in the workforce development program. It's a three-week intensive for (mainly) men who, no matter how hard they've tried, can't seem to get out of their own way when it comes to keeping a job.

Self-sabotage. My mind pinged.

I asked him, John was his name, if it'd be overstepping for me to come and speak to these guys. Specifically, on self-sabotage.

Parentheses formed at the corners of his mouth. "No," he said. "Not at all!"

Next thing I knew, I was scheduled to give a speech at the end of the month.

March 6, 2023 (what would have been my dad's sixtieth birthday, oddly enough)

The time between writing in the morning and speech rehearsal in the evening was filled with QLA—cold-calling business owners, trying to find that one *Motivated Seller* willing to let us buy his business with his own money.

I'll be frank with you. I made 200 calls a day, every day, come hell or high water. But my motivation for QLA—despite the fact that I was in business with *The Trillion Dollar Man,* Mr. Peña—had begun to wane.

I'm crazy, I know.

Try to see it from my perspective. The only thing that was "working" for me was speaking. From being asked to speak to high school kids about turning adversity to advantage to helping men at Mel Trotter Ministries stop self-sabotage to winning freaking Table Topics Championships. Speaking was working for me.

And the more I spoke, the more I learned about myself and my story.

The more I learned about myself and my story, the more I was able to write.

The more I was able to write, the closer I got to knowing the answer to the trillion-dollar question on my blackboard. But all of that came to a halt when I received the following email from Mr. Peña that morning:

> ***MENTEES:***
>
> ***UNLIKE MOST OF U, THAT I AM CHAIR OF UR (R) DEAL – U DON'T LISTEN & WATCH ME DAILY, ON MY THE VARIOUS OUTLETS! AS U ALL KNOW, FROM HEARING/SEEING WEBINARS AT THE SEMINAR - EVERY SINGLE SUPER SUCCESSFUL MENTEE, U HEARD IN WEBINARS & IN PERSON SAID, THEY CONTINUE 2 LISTEN/WATCH ME DAILY! SUM ACTUALLY DO IT WID THEIR KIDS! FUNNY, AS U HAVE HEARD ME SAY, I STILL LISTEN/WATCH MYSELF DAILY!***
>
> ***THIS YR 2023, I AM EVALUATING, WHERE I AM STAYING CHAIR & WHERE I AM GOING 2 RESIGN! THE ONLY REAL BENCHMARK WILL B DEALS COMPLETED! NOT***

LOI'S! NOT OFFERS MADE! NOT TERM SHEETS! AS U ALL KNOW, I AM REDUCING MY CHAIRS & 2023 WILL B A FINAL PUSH, 2 ENTER MY 80'S GRACEFULLY!
2 UR QL IN LIFE & BIS!
DAN

My blood ran cold.

Sure, I had a few prospects lined up. But we weren't even close to presenting an offer or signing an LOI, (Letter of Intent). Much less, completing a deal.

That email changed my trajectory in a major way—the wrong way. I was in danger of losing Mr. Peña. And you heard the man, the only thing that would prevent that from happening would be getting a deal done.

That day, I put Mr. Peña above everything. This book, God, you name it. I did not want to commit the greatest act of self-sabotage by losing *The Trillion Dollar Man* as my Chairman.

Temptation.

SECTION IX: ATONEMENT WITH THE FATHER

The center point of the journey, and all the previous steps the hero has taken along their quest have moved towards this moment. It is now that the hero must confront and be initiated by whatever holds the ultimate power in his or her life.

Change Your Story—Part Four

March 10, 2023

That morning I gave a speech to a small group of high schoolers at Grand Rapids Union High School. Anyone from the area knows the kind of kid that attends Union High is the kind of kid whose life is absorbed by adversity. My goal was simple: help them turn life's adversities into their advantage.

In other words, they had a choice to make. They could be the victim, or they could be the hero. But here's the rub, and this is what I told them: "You can't do it on your own. Would Harry Potter, Katniss Everdeen, or Luke Skywalker have been able to do it on their own? No! They had Hagrid, Haymitch, and Obi Wan Kenobi, didn't they? Victims do it alone. Heroes do it with a guide—and what better guide than God?"

I didn't care that I was speaking at a public school. I came to help these kids. I came to give them the truth; to show them The Way to change their story.

Speaking of stories, I told them the story about Mr. Jones and the importance of putting God first. I told them how each of them had a gift; how I used my gift of writing to help my friend Jaide; and how they'll never go broke using their gift to help those who are *broken*—because those moments are worth far more than money—so go all-in. And lastly, I told them to run *their* race; walking them through the last indoor meet of the season less than a month before then. I told them as soon as they start to compare themselves to, or compete against others, they're already a victim; they lose the power to turn life's adversities to their advantage.

"You kids still hold the pen." I said. "Your story isn't over, but you can't rewrite what's already been written. So, get out there and start that new chapter…*today.*"

The Golden Calf—Part Four

March 13, 2023

I was still riding the high of the speech I gave at Union High, and I had found another *Motivated Seller*—he and his partners owned a small, assisted living facility outside of Joliet, Illinois. My CFO and I had a Zoom call scheduled with the business owner later that day to listen to what he and his partners were looking for in an offer. That meeting was going to be a kind gesture more than anything. You've probably surmised we were going to present a 100% seller-financed deal—and you'd be right.

With a few hours to kill before the call, I went to the track. My calf was feeling the best it'd felt since the initial strain in early December. And with the outdoor track season a little over six-weeks away, I needed to start pushing my training a little harder.[36]

The weather in Michigan, however, kept me indoors that day.

---

[36] Some sprinters might disagree, but I think the outdoor season is more taxing than the indoor season, for a couple reasons. 1) You're outdoors, which invites windy days, excessive heat at times, and rain—all of which aren't 100% ideal conditions. The indoor season negates the elements. 2) The outdoor season is on a 400-meter track. Most indoor tracks are 200-300 meters in length; the turns are sharper, the straightaways are shorter—both variables are more considerable than a non-sprinter might think.

Sixty-meter sprints on a curve were on the docket that day—the same workout that caused my injury back in December. Back to the scene of the crime.

I set my Bluetooth timing gates at the thirty and sixty meter marks.

I took a deep breath, rolled over my front knee and put on speed.

PING! went the timing gate at thirty meters.

POW! went my calf about ten meters later.

Self-Sabotaging Men are kind of like serial killers. They just can't help themselves. For whatever reason, they have to go back to the scene of the crime.

The Golden Calf—Part Five

March 20, 2023

The business owner in Joliet ended up not being as motivated as we thought. He, like the first, wanted $1M at the close. He and his partners sold to another buyer.

Another dead deal. Talk about adding insult to injury.

With my tail tucked between my legs, I limped gingerly down the stairs to the basement, (I was just one week removed from restraining my calf) to put the finishing touches on a PowerPoint deck I would use as a reference for my upcoming keynote at Mel Trotter Ministries ten days from then.

The content was good. I had my three steps, the same steps I spoke to the Union High kids about. But there was something missing, something powerful. It felt like it needed a *Deus Ex Machina,* or some kind of climactic moment, to really drive the point home. These guys weren't so different from the Israelites wandering in the wilderness. They were stuck in self-sabotage, looking for answers in all the wrong places, worshiping—

That's when it hit me.

It was that same, voice-like feeling that came over me before injuring my calf the first time in early December. But this voice, or feeling, whatever it was, wasn't pulling me away from the track. No. It was pushing me *toward* it. I can best describe it as an idea that hijacked my consciousness.

Going to the track that morning and sprinting was all I

could think about.

Nope. I thought. I was one-week removed from *another* calf strain, thank you very much. *Not doing it.* I was so discouraged and fed up with the recurring injury, I had barely started the return-to-play process.

But that voice-like feeling waxed hot, like God's finger touched my heart.

Half an hour later I was at the track in a full sweat.

I did some easy jogging.

I did a few drills; marching, skipping, high-knees, nothing that irritated my injured calf.

I felt good.

I went through an entire warm-up without pain or soreness.

I chalked up the day as a win.

I walked over to the bench and sat down. I was sweating on the outside. On the inside? I was on fire. The heat was overwhelming, like I was ablaze.

I felt like Mario after getting a Superstar—I felt invincible.

But feeling that way didn't quell my fear of doing what I knew I had to do that day.

In sterquiliniis invenitur.

This is crazy. Was on repeat in my head as I set up the Bluetooth timing gates for a flying ten-meter.[37]

When everything was set up, I took a moment to gather myself on the bench. Sweat dripped off the blade of my nose like a leaky faucet.

My heartbeat was in my throat.

My eyes filled with water, teary with fear.

My heels tapped the track like mini-jackhammers.

My hands trembled as I slipped my spikes on.

---

[37] Basically, a forty-meter dash. The last ten meters between the thirty and forty marks are where the Bluetooth timing gates are placed; that's the zone that's timed. It's a good metric for one's top speed.

I took a deep breath and walked toward the starting line, stopping a few meters behind it.

"This is crazy," I said, making a full circle with my neck. It popped like champagne corks. I took another deep breath. "Get ready for a miracle."

I bounced toward the start line.

Before I knew it, I was running.

Ten meters. No pain.

Twenty meters. No pain.

I'm running. I thought. *Holy sh—*

PING! went the Bluetooth timer at forty meters.

I decelerated slowly and deliberately before finally coming to a stop. I whirled around, placing my hands on my hips. "I can't believe I did that."

My time was 1.04 seconds—just two-hundredths shy of my all-time personal record, 1.02.

I bit down hard on my lower lip, clapping hard. "Okay," I said, nodding to myself as I walked back to the bench.

I just sprinted full speed on a strained calf, I thought, then laughed.

I knew I was going to do another rep.

Doing so any other time before this would have been typical self-sabotaging behavior.

But this time was different.

This wasn't self-sabotage.

This was The Way out of self-sabotage; into self-mastery.

I wasn't in control, *He* was.

When I was weak, *He* was strong.

After a five-minute break, I walked to the starting line. This time, with confidence.

I pushed myself away from the line and I was off.

Ten meters.

Twenty meters.

Thirty.

Forty.

PING!

The fastest I had ever run: 1.01 seconds—22.15 miles per hour.

I laughed like an exuberant child. My eyes welled. At that moment, I realized that voice-like feeling was God talking to me the past few months and all the years prior.

When I wrote my first story, that was Him.

When Jesus visited my dad and me, that was Him.

When I first saw Tiffany, that was Him.

When I spoke at QLA Graduation Night at Guthrie Castle, that was Him.

When I knew I shouldn't have sprinted that morning in December, but did anyway, that was Him.

Jesus was desperately trying to get my attention with calf injury after calf injury. It's as if He was saying: "Son! Enough is enough! The Golden Calf has injured your soul for far too long! Now it's injuring your body! Please, Son, run to *me!* I know what you've been looking for since your father died! I am He! I am The Way, the truth, and the life, no one comes to the Father except through *me!"*

Yep. I thought on my drive home. *That's what my presentation was missing.*

The power to change my story.

But having the power and using it are two very different things.

Jesus gave me the power to change my story. Jesus made my injured calf as good as gold. Now I needed to hold my end of the bargain. I had to burn my Golden Calf.

I finally knew what it meant to put God first, now I had to do it.

Who Are You More Afraid to Lose?

March 22, 2023

Despite having my "burning bush" moment with God Himself, I met with Father Stephen, a priest from our local church two days later.

I laid out the whole scenario for him.

To the left was potentially millions, if not billions, of dollars with Mr. Peña.

To the right was…speaking, with no money attached to it whatsoever. Sure, I was being presented with opportunities galore, but none were paid.

The same couldn't be said for QLA and closing our first deal, despite having made thousands (yes, thousands, easily) of cold calls to business owners across the Midwest.

"Which begs the question," I said, then made a *pffi!* sound. "Is that [all the speaking success and engagements] a sign I need to keep following Him? And if it is, perhaps the better question is: who are you more afraid to lose, Hunter? God, or Mr. Peña?"

Folds formed on Fr. Stephen's forehead. "That's a great question," he said. "Y'know, before I went to seminary school, I was crazy about a girl named Josie. I wanted very much to pursue a relationship with her, but I felt God calling me to be a priest. This went on for a while, and it was really stressing me out. So, one day I finally prayed on it and said:

'Okay God, you can have Josie.' and as soon as I made the decision…" Fr. Stephen's hands floated up just above his head, and then they dropped into a sweeping motion down either side of him. "I felt an overwhelming sense of peace about it. I went to seminary school and the rest is history."

"And you're happy?" I asked. "With your decision to become a priest?"

"Oh yes, very much so," Father said, then swung a look over his shoulder. The clock read ten minutes till nine. Father looked back at me, patting the armrests on either side of him. "You'll have to excuse me, I have a mass to say."

"Of course," I said, and thanked him for his time.

"Let's pray," he said. "Lord Jesus, we pray that you give Hunter the wisdom to know what is right and the courage to do it. Hunter? Do you have anything you'd like to pray for?"

I cleared my throat and said: "Lord Jesus, I ask that you continue to help me find the words so those I speak to are able to bridge the gap from self-sabotage to self-mastery."

"Amen," Fr. Stephen said, jutting his lower lip out and nodding. "From self-sabotage to self-mastery. I like that."

Self-Realization—Part Two

When I got home from my meeting with Fr. Stephen, I threw on my favorite three-piece suit—white shirt, charcoal black vest and coat, completed with a blood-red tie.

I went down into the gym in my basement, attached my phone to a tripod and pressed RECORD.

"Hello Mr. Peña," I said, taking a seat on a plyo-box, checking my watch. "It is Wednesday, March twenty-second, twelve thirty PM eastern standard time. You probably don't remember, during our private time, when you had asked me, 'How can I help you?' as you were sifting through my papers and my files and my questions I had written to you before I came to Guthrie, but I said: 'Whatever you're looking at, Mr. Peña, you can just wipe your ass with it because that's about all it's good for."

I shrugged. "Why did I do that?" I sighed, then stomped my right foot to the beat of the following: "Because it was a self...sabotaging...activity! And I didn't even know it. I couldn't even help myself. Why? Because Default is a mother effing b****[38]! That's why."

I winced, then continued, sharing the stories of my early years with him.

How I felt unfavored and unworthy and like a victim.

How so many children and adults feel the same.

How my story, my Default, kept me stuck—even

[38] My attempt at keeping the language light.

successfully.

Then I shared the story about Mrs. Schmitz; when I first knew I was a writer. I stood up from the plyo-box and removed my jacket. "Now, I understand, Mr. Peña, if you're disgusted with that sob story. I understand, believe me, I get it," I plopped my jacket back on the plyo-box behind me. "But the truth of the matter is, when I got to be a teenager, I didn't know how to handle real adversity, and so I Defaulted back to being a victim," I rolled up my left sleeve, revealing my tattoo-covered forearm. "Too many times, I'd come home after school, run upstairs and lock myself in my closet. I'd straighten out one of our wire clothes hangers and—" I made slashing gestures over the tattoos. "Hence the tattoos to cover them. Why did I do that? I'm sure you remember the story I told about my father on Graduation Night."

I took a seat again, rolling down and buttoning my sleeve. "I share that with you not for your sympathy, Mr. Peña." I shook my head. "No. Far from it. I share that with you because there are way too many kids and adults out there suffering from anxiety and depression and Defaulting back to their self-sabotaging activities because of sh** like *that* that happens in their life. And I want them to know that even though their story might not make sense at times, God has a plan for them. And that plan includes the power to change their story.

"So, that begs the question: How does it work?" I shrugged, and said: "Well, it's really simple: One: put God first. Two: go all-in. Three: run *your* race." I said, then recalled the six-hour phone call with Mr. Jones. I told him about the time when, though briefly, I had gone all-in on writing for my high school friend, Jaide. And I told him his advice to join Toastmasters has opened up a plethora of speaking opportunities, saying: "I wouldn't have known that I had the gift of speaking not been for you, Mr. Peña, and now I'm going all-in on it. You helped me change my story, and when I changed my story, I changed my life."

I relived the recent memory of my last indoor meet at Grand Valley on February 17, 2023, the Toastmasters Area Championship the day after, and the run *your* race revelation that came as a result of those events.

Before concluding, I took a deep breath and said: "I'm not quitting QLA. I'm just getting started. I have clarity. One of your favorite mentees, Dan Lok, says, 'clarity is power' and with that power comes the ability and the opportunity to help kids and adults stop self-sabotage. I'm going all in on this, and whether or not you want to help, or join, is irrelevant, Mr. Peña. But, had I not come to you, Mr. Peña, I would not have realized this."

I paused, nodding affirmingly to myself. "You see, the bridge from self-sabotage to self-mastery is self-realization. And now that I've realized who I am and what I need to do, I'm going all in. I'm gonna run *my* race."

I put the video in an email and before I pressed SEND, I sighed, looked up and said: "Okay God, you can have Mr. Peña."

Atonement with the Father.

SECTION X: THE ALL IS LOST MOMENT

The final crisis for the hero.

Self-Realization—Part Three

March 25, 2023

The Toastmasters Table Topics Division Championship. The winner from each division would advance to the District i.e., state Championship in late April.

"Hunter Charneski," the contest emcee said. "Who is more likely to be successful, the Jack-of-All-Trades, or the Master-of-One?"

God knew I had been the former my entire life.

I knew I was going to be the latter for the rest of it.

"If I had to say who is more likely to be successful between the Jack-of-All-Trades and the Master-of-One," I said. "I would have to say the Master-of-One, and here's why: I knew I was a writer for a long time, since I was eleven, in fact, but I didn't pursue it. *Why not?* you might be wondering. It was because it didn't look like *success* to me. And I didn't find it to be particularly rewarding. So, I stuffed it down, barely touching it for the next twenty years. *Big* mistake.

"It was only until the summer of 2020 when I decided to finally stop running from writing. I've written almost every single day since then. And here's the cool part: writing has made me more articulate and what's more, it's been the tool to help dig up the fossil inside of me that is my *voice.*

"Had I not done one thing, writing every day, then I would not be here on this stage to share that story with all of you. I am a living, breathing example of the Master-of-One being more successful than the Jack-of-All-Trades—and that's clinical, not conceited. Thank you."

First-place.

I was on my way to the District Championship.

My All is Lost Moment

March 27, 2023

Two-days later, Mr. Peña's response to my video hit my inbox:

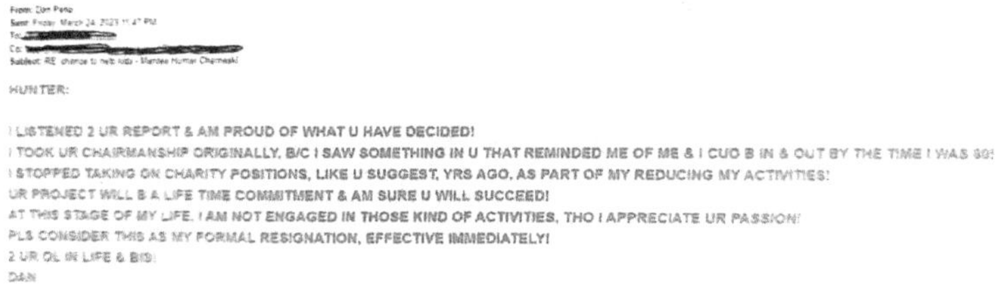

From: Dan Peña
Sent: Friday, March 24, 2023 11:47 PM
To:
Cc:
Subject: RE: [illegible]

HUNTER:

I LISTENED 2 UR REPORT & AM PROUD OF WHAT U HAVE DECIDED!
I TOOK UR CHAIRMANSHIP ORIGINALLY, B/C I SAW SOMETHING IN U THAT REMINDED ME OF ME & I CUD B IN & OUT BY THE TIME I WAS 80!
I STOPPED TAKING ON CHARITY POSITIONS, LIKE U SUGGEST, YRS AGO, AS PART OF MY REDUCING MY ACTIVITIES!
UR PROJECT WILL B A LIFE TIME COMMITMENT & AM SURE U WILL SUCCEED!
AT THIS STAGE OF MY LIFE, I AM NOT ENGAGED IN THOSE KIND OF ACTIVITIES, THO I APPRECIATE UR PASSION!
PLS CONSIDER THIS AS MY FORMAL RESIGNATION, EFFECTIVE IMMEDIATELY!
2 UR QL IN LIFE & BIS!
DAN

Image 6: Mr. Peña's resignation email, source: Hunter M. Charneski

After Bill Galik's original investment in me of more than $30K; after traveling to Scotland and returning home with The Trillion Dollar Man as my Chairman; after the countless hours of work, hundreds of rejections, being laughed out of offices by accountants, and thousands of cold calls in search of the one deal that would change our lives forever, it was over.

As I reread the email several times, I was torn.

It felt good to know that Mr. Peña was proud of me, I won't lie.

It felt better knowing that someone as successful as Mr. Peña saw himself in *me.*

QLA is designed to be a three-to-four-year sprint. My project, as Mr. Peña alluded to, was going to be a lifetime commitment—I was going to run *my* race. I was going to follow my passion, something I know Mr. Peña appreciates more than anyone.

But as good as I tried to make myself feel, I couldn't argue with reality.

I lost Mr. Peña as my Chairman.

I walked away from the Trillion Dollar Man.

That was my All Is Lost Moment.

SECTION XI: THE EPIPHANAL MOMENT

The hero attains what he set out for when the journey began.

Self-Mastery

I went for a walk an hour later.

I needed to lick my wounds.

I needed to digest the frog I just swallowed.

I needed to interrogate myself.

I needed answers.

Boy, did I get one.

I remember turning the corner on the sidewalk that hugged our neighbor's well-kept lawn. I was staring at the gray lines in the concrete, scorning myself with harsh thoughts.

What have you done? I mean really. Do you know how many thousands *of QLA mentees and devotees would have* killed *to have Mr. Peña as their Chairman? And you just walked away from him? And for what? Writing and speaking? A book-and-a-speech for God's sa—*

I stopped walking.

My eyes widened.

"But most kids don't follow their passion." My mind replayed what Mr. Peña said on *London Real. "It's their* Default...*And Default's a bi***!"*

That's it. Default. That's the answer to the trillion-dollar question. That's why we sabotage ourselves. I said so in my video to Mr. Peña but didn't realize it until that exact moment—The Epiphanal Moment.

It was like lighting a match in a dark place.

Walking away from Mr. Peña wasn't self-sabotage. It

was the exact opposite.

One doesn't simply depart from *The Trillion Dollar Man* without knowing exactly who they are—that's self-realization.

That's *self-mastery.*

Had I stayed with Mr. Peña and gone through with our plans for world-domination in HealthCare, *that* would have been—and I mean this technically—the most successful act of self-sabotage ever.

The headlines in heaven would have read:

HUNTER CHARNESKI, THE MAN WHO—YET AGAIN—IS *SUCCESSFULLY STUCK!*

That's what the headline *would have* read, but won't. I had achieved what I set out to do.

I made Mr. Peña, my mentor. And he helped me, in the most peculiar way, put an end to my self-sabotage. I wasn't dismantled by my Default—I redefined it.

This book is literal proof of that.

The Epiphanal Moment.

SECTION XII: REFUSAL OF THE RETURN

The stage of the hero's journey in which the hero refuses their duty to return home and bestow their newfound wisdom upon the rest of humanity.

After the Wilderness

March 29, 2023

Two days had passed since my epiphany.

The only problem was, I wasn't sure where to go from there. The journey had seemingly gone completely internal, which isn't all bad, except for the fact that life is a great deal external as well.

I don't know what possessed me to do this, but I fished out the laptop I used during my short sprint in insurance.[39] It had been collecting dust in the drawer in my desk since I left for QLA. I opened it up and—again, I must have been possessed—checked an old email account I hadn't used in over a year.

At the top of my inbox was, as fate would have it, Steven Pressfield's weekly newsletter, *Writing Wednesday.* The email, just a few hours old, had the subject line: *After the Wilderness.*

> *Our passage through the Wilderness may involve action worthy of the next John Wick movie. We may survive*

[39] It probably sounds weird, but I had two laptops; one for work and one for writing. Having one strictly for writing prevented me from being distracted by work stuff.

IEDs in Afghanistan, divorces in Reno, stretches in Joliet or in a cubicle at Facebook. We may find ourselves brawling in bars in Ibiza, pursuing lovers across the Pampas in Argentina. We may wake up with strange tattoos, or beside even stranger bed-mates. Entire decades can go missing during our Wilderness Passage.

*But when we finally turn the corner—**when we reach our All Is Lost Moment, followed by our Epiphanal Moment**—all that adventure shifts.*

It goes inside.

Our life becomes now, about the work—the work we've been running away from all that time in the wilderness.

Dalton Trumbo wrote his best stuff in the bathtub. Churchill the same. Marcel Proust barely got out of bed. Even Hunter Thompson, mythology aside, took his orange juice straight when he settled down at the keyboard.

Me? The odometer on my '65 Chevy van ticked over the six-digit mark so many times I can't remember them all. That

> *was during my hero's journey.*
>
> *Now on my Artist's journey I barely drive to the grocery store.*

You can't make this stuff up.

Thinking Pressfield's email was nothing short of divine timing, I figured I'd send him a note back:

> *If I may, what comes after the epiphanal moment?*

Why not? I thought.

Pressfield didn't know me. Maybe he'd reply, but probably not.

His response came within minutes, (must've been a slow day at the office).

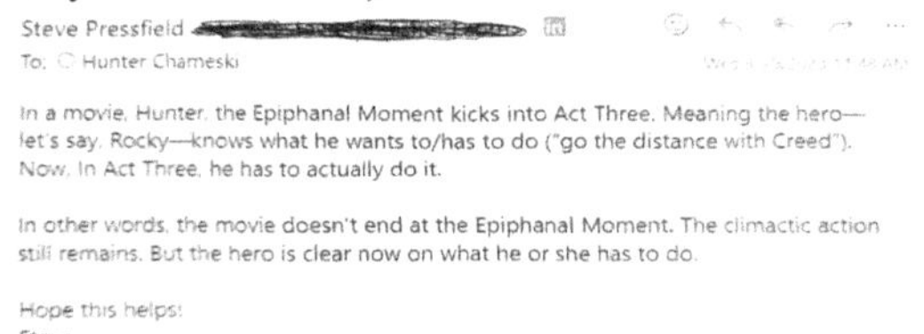

Steve Pressfield

To: Hunter Chameski

In a movie, Hunter, the Epiphanal Moment kicks into Act Three. Meaning the hero—let's say, Rocky—knows what he wants to/has to do ("go the distance with Creed"). Now, In Act Three, he has to actually do it.

In other words, the movie doesn't end at the Epiphanal Moment. The climactic action still remains. But the hero is clear now on what he or she has to do.

Hope this helps!

Steve

Image 7: An email received from Steven Pressfield, source: Hunter M. Charneski

It did help, thanks Steve.

I'll be honest. I just wanted to write.

My adventure shifted, it went inside.

But, as Pressfield said in his email, I knew what I had to do—even if I didn't want to.

Refusal of the Return.

SECTION XIII: MAGIC FLIGHT

The stage where the hero may need to escape, literally or metaphorically, with The Ultimate Boon, as he leaves the Extraordinary World and returns to the Ordinary World.

Motivated Sellers

March 30, 2023

The next day, multiple emails flooded my inbox from *Motivated Sellers.*

Each note read similar to the one below:

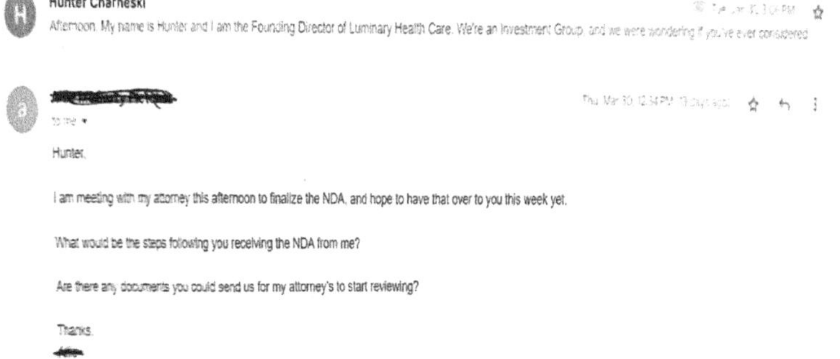

Hunter Charneski

Afternoon. My name is Hunter and I am the Founding Director of Luminary Health Care. We're an Investment Group, and we were wondering if you've ever considered

Thu, Mar 30, 12:34 PM

Hunter,

I am meeting with my attorney this afternoon to finalize the NDA, and hope to have that over to you this week yet.

What would be the steps following you receiving the NDA from me?

Are there any documents you could send us for my attorney's to start reviewing?

Thanks,

Image 8: An email received from a Motivated Seller, source: Hunter M. Charneski

I was tempted to move forward.

Sure, Mr. Peña resigned. But how hard would it be to find another chairman, given the track record of the rest of my Dream Team?

Speaking of, my Dream Team was none the wiser of his resignation (yet).

Maybe I could find Mr. Peña's replacement before informing my Dream Team of his resignation? I could do it.

I could definitely do—

Then I felt that black column of dread creeping up my spine.

I knew whose voice that was now.

I wasn't going back down that road.

I sent an email that day notifying my Dream Team of not only Mr. Peña's resignation, but my own.

Magic Flight.

SECTION XIV: RESCUE FROM WITHOUT

When the hero requires aid from a powerful external benefactor to escape the realm of the supernatural and return home.

An Act of God

April 4, 2023

I was driving home from a meeting when it happened.

It was a quarter till seven.

The sun had begun to retreat toward the horizon.

The sky was the color of bruised skin.

I had the cruise set at seventy-seven, my right hand held the wheel at five o'clock, and my left hand idled on my lap.

Then the highway waxed from charcoal gray to white, my knuckles mirrored the color as I death-gripped the steering wheel.

The hell? I thought. *It's not cold enough to snow.*

The white bits became more coarse and greater in number.

When I looked out into the distance, the traffic had slowed to a crawl.

There was nothing but a swath of red brake lights ahead.

The white coarse bits on the highway were growing, both in size and in number.

I was coming up on an overpass. By the time I reached it, the highway was white as a sheet, like a road of crushed diamonds. Cars and trucks and semis were cramped bumper-to-bumper underneath the overpass. I just kept driving, wondering why they were—

THWAP!

A crack split down the center of my windshield.

A baseball-sized hailstone idled on my wipers.

THWAP!

Another hailstone struck my car, this one even bigger, denting the roof.

THWAP-THWAP-THWAP!

My car was getting pelted.

I felt like the poor son-of-a-gun driving the ball-collector at the driving range, only this time, God and all His angels were seemingly teeing off on me from the clouds above. Within seconds my windshield looked like a meandering silver river with glassy tributaries stretching from top to bottom.

I was caught in a full-blown hailstorm.

The scene was biblical.

I flicked my right blinker on, started to pull over as I came up on the next overpass when God's voice struck me again. Like the downpour outside my car, a rainfall of peace washed over me. It was an undeniable feeling of *everything was going to be okay; He was telling me to trust Him.*

Despite the fact my roof was probably cratered worse than the surface of the moon, I filled my foot with lead and punched the gas.

Things got worse before they got better.

Another crack at the bottom of the windshield didn't give me much hope that it'd be able to hold. My roof sounded like it was taking a shower of empty bullet casings.

Then in an instant, the clanging and banging turned to a soft fan of rain, the kind that lulls you to sleep.

It was over.

I had made it through.

"Can't wait to write about this one," I said just louder than a whisper.

I had followed God's voice, and He led me out of the storm.

I should mention that it seemed God rewarded such faith.

The insurance company mailed us a check in the amount of $2,500.00[40]—enough money to make the necessary repairs *and pay Tiffany's and my mortgage*.

I'm not too far removed from the insurance industry to have forgotten this sort of thing is categorized as "An Act of God."

Rescue from Without.

[40] Mind you, Tiffany and I were struggling for cash; walking away from Mr. Peña, though the right thing to do, wasn't exactly lucrative.

SECTION XV: A GIFT FOR THE PEOPLE

The hero returns to the Ordinary World, bestowing the wisdom he's learned on his journey.

Put God First—Part Two

April 29, 2023

The Toastmasters Table Topics District Championship.

"Hunter Charneski," the Contest Chair said. "What is the most amazing success you've experienced that you've never told anyone? Here is your chance."

I wrung my hands together and bowed my head.

I squinted hard at the maroon and black argyle patterns on the carpet just beyond the stage I stood on. Jaide's story leapt into my consciousness immediately, marinating for a second or two, then fell away in favor of something else. I was ablaze. I felt His presence. It was as if He said: "*This* is what you're going to tell them."

I lifted my head, looked out at the audience, opened my mouth and said: "The most amazing success I have *ever* experienced is putting God first…"

Image 9: Me being presented with the 1st Place trophy and certificate at the Toastmasters Table Topics District Championship on April 29, 2023, with (from left to right) our local club's members: Pamela, Lisa, and John. source: Hunter M. Charneski

Put God first and a District Championship for the smallest Toastmasters club in the state?

Yeah, I'd say that qualifies as a Gift for the People.

SECTION XVI: MASTER OF TWO WORLDS

The hero is back in the Ordinary World, but he is not the same. He was a novice in the Ordinary World before the journey began. Now he is a master of it, able to assert himself in a meaningful way.

Do What You Do Best

May 4, 2023

My phone buzzed. It was a text from John, my old boss at the financial firm.

"Hi Hunter, how's it going? Hey, I wanted to reach out to you. I'd like to see how your career is progressing and I have an interesting idea. Let's do lunch next week."

May 11, 2023

Our lunch appointment was at a small bistro in downtown Grand Rapids. A hipster joint; contemporary, but laissez-faire. You know the kind.

"How are you?" John said, pushing himself to stand as I approached our table.

"I'm well," I said, shaking his hand before unbuttoning my suit jacket and sitting down. "And you?"

"Good, good," he said. "Better than I was, that's for sure."

I reached for the glass of ice water in front of me, pausing halfway toward my mouth. "What do you mean?"

"See these?" John said, pointing to a couple scars near his temple. "Scars from surgery back in December. I got real sick."

"I'm sorry to hear that, John," I said, setting the glass back. "But you're okay now?"

"Yeah," he said with a sigh, passing a hand down his tie. "I'm good."

"Doesn't sound like it."

He frowned, tossing his head left and right. "After I got out of the hospital, I asked myself: 'What the hell are you doing?' I haven't accomplished nearly what I should have by now. I'm gonna be *sixty* next month, you know that right?"

I nodded.

"I left the firm shortly after."

"Did you?" I said. "What're you doing now? Still in the financial industry?"

"Oh yes," he said, leaning back in his seat. "I'll be in this industry till the day I walk off this earth," he said, pushing a hand through the air. "So fill me in, what's going on with you? How're things? What're you doing now?"

"Writing and speaking," I said.

"You've always been a tremendous speaker," John said.

"You're very kind," I said. "Thank you."

"Who're you speaking to?"

"Adults and children, mostly," I said, then swept my hand back and forth from left to right. "On one end of the spectrum, I help children see life's adversities as their advantage, and on the other end, I help adults bridge the gap from self-sabotage to self-mastery."

"Very good," John said, nodding.

"What about you?" I asked, frowning. "You're no longer with the firm, but you're still in the industry—"

"That's right," John said with a nod. "Which is why I wanted to meet with you today. I've found a company that's willing to fund what we talked about—"

"What do you mean?"

John furrowed his eyebrows at me. "C'mon man you

know what I mean."

"J. Smith and Associates?"

John nodded.

"What's that got to do with me?" I asked.

"I've seen what you're capable of," John said.

"I appreciate that," I said. "But since the last time I saw you, God has humbled me. I'm a writer and I'm a speaker, John. I'm not selling life insurance anymore."

John frowned, taking a moment to rearrange his silverware. "I'm not asking you to sell life insurance…"

I said nothing.

"I need you to sell the vision," he shook a fist at me. "Come in, *do what you do best*, get the team going. You'll collect a percentage of their production. I'm not asking for a lot of your time."

I pondered it for a moment, then asked: "How're your books coming?"

John squinted hard as if the question soured him. Perhaps it did. "Why would you ask me that?"

"You know exactly why I asked you that, John," I said, jamming my index finger down into the table. "You've always wanted to be a writer."

He passed a hand down his face, shook his head and said, "I took all three of 'em out just last night and laid them all on my desk. Not one is finished."

I shook a finger at him, leaning over the table. "Do you think it's a coincidence that you brought those out *last night* and then I asked about them *today?*"

"No." John said. "No, I don't think it's a coincidence. I just can't finish them, for whatever reason I just can't. I got too many goals I haven't achieved yet, things I thought I'd have by now, money I ought to—"

"John." I said. "Have you ever considered that maybe the reason you haven't achieved any of the material things you desire is because you haven't completed your spiritual assignment yet? Perhaps you won't realize all the success you want until you sit down and finish those books."

He lowered his gaze for a moment, blinked twice, then looked back up at me.

"You are a writer, John," I said. "Do what *you do* best."

I never saw John again, hopefully because he's writing, hopefully because he's found The Way out of self-sabotage, too. Hopefully because he, too, has become a Master of Two Worlds.

SECTION XVII: FREEDOM TO LIVE

The hero's journey is complete. The hero has revivified his father, and in doing so no longer regrets the past nor fears the future. The hero is finally free.

The Way—Part Six

For seventeen years I wondered why my dad didn't want me there when he died.

I thought the answer was revealed to me during my time at QLA, but that wasn't it.

My dad didn't want me to see him die with regrets, but not in the way I originally thought. It was way deeper than that, and when it hit me, it felt like a cold knife touched the nape of my neck.

Summer 2023 (I don't remember exactly when)

I was listening to a podcast in our basement as I did some light stretching and breathing exercises before going to the track.

The podcast was a Dr. Jordan B. Peterson compilation of motivational quotes.

I, like Dr. Peterson and Steven Pressfield, see life through the lens of a story—a hero's journey.

Dr. Peterson spoke on, and I'm paraphrasing here, a particular motif in the hero's journey where the hero must go down into the abyss, or the *Belly of the Whale* (in my case, going into business with Mr. Peña) and revivify, or give new life to, his father (Simba and Mufasa, Tony and Howard

Stark, Luke Skywalker and Darth Vader are classic examples). In doing so, the hero gives new life to his father *through* him.

"I am The Way and the truth and the life. No one comes to the father except through me." – John 14:6

That's when it hit me—the night Jesus visited my dad and me.

That night, Jesus asked my dad to do something that took me thirty-two years to do.

He asked my dad to put God first—even before me, his firstborn.

Revelation rained down on me.

It all made sense now.

If I was there the night my dad died, I would have seen him die with regret—the Ultimate Regret of not finding The Way back to him, *through Him.*

If I had the closure of being there the night he died, I never would have wondered, and wandered, for as long as I did in the wilderness. I never would have endured the pain of self-sabotage for two decades that led me to look where I least wanted to: going all-in on my gift and revivifying my earthly father by being reborn through my heavenly Father. That's why my dad didn't want me there the night he died. Clarity.

My dad bet on me; he trusted Him.

Jesus knew I would eventually find Him.

Jesus knew when I did, I would become Batman.

No, that's not what happened. I didn't become anything, or anyone. I simply remembered who I was all along—a child of God with a gift of writing; a gift to me and from me to you.

Self-realization.

In doing so, Jesus knew I would run *my* race so you could redefine your Default of the Self-Sabotaging Man, burn your Golden Calf and realize who you've been all along: a writer, songwriter, visionary, breakdancer, gym owner, and go all-in on that; changing your story in the process.

Because when you change your story, you change your life.

This is The Way out of self-sabotage; into self-mastery.

Freedom to Live.

PART THREE: SELF-MASTERY

"It is finished." – John 19:30

SECTION I: WHAT IS SELF-MASTERY?

What is Self-Mastery?—Part One

Self-mastery isn't when you master yourself; it's when all things that were your master no longer are.

What is Self-Mastery?—Part Two

Self-mastery is knowing what to ignore.

What is Self-Mastery?—Part Three

Doing the same things differently, that's what self-mastery is.

Take me for example. I'm writing what I'm supposed to be writing—narrative nonfiction for now, that horror novel someday soon, don't you worry—and I'm doing it the way I'm supposed to be. I'm not punting my job or my marriage just so I can have any and all my time dedicated to the craft. But I'm not sitting on the sidelines, either, only writing when the mood strikes.

I've found the—another cliché, I'm afraid—*happy medium.* There is such a thing as balance. I don't care what anyone tells you. In the past, I either wrote too much—self-sabotage by overidentification—or too little—self-sabotage by sacrificing my gift for success. Now, I write the right amount, and I write what's right for me, when it's right for me to write. *Hey-o!*

I'm a writer. I'm doing the same thing I've always done, I'm just doing the same thing differently. That's what self-mastery is.

Get Your Act Together

How many times have you heard the phrase: "Get your act together"?

Have you ever asked yourself why that phrase exists? Or others like it, such as:

- "It builds character."
- "Step into your role."
- "Start a new chapter."
- "Get your story straight."
- "Turn the page."

Those metaphors are all predicated on story.

Why?

I think it comes from some kind of deeply implicit, primordial understanding we possess. In other words, we can't help but see our lives as stories.

Stories guide us; they're how we make sense of things.

If someone says to you: "Get your act together!" What that means, I think, is that it's become apparent to them you're not playing the role you're supposed to; the character you're playing is the victim instead of the hero; you're not accepting the Call to Adventure; you're not going all-in on your gift; you're not being a Grimit.

We've been telling stories for as long as humankind has been around. It's safe to assume then, because of our proclivity to be captivated by stories, our lives are no different—our lives are stories. If that's the case—and that's been the entire point I've been trying to make, if you hadn't noticed—as characters, we possess the power to change our story.

So, get your act together.

Hedgehogs

"The fox knows many tricks; but the hedgehog knows one big one." — Archilochus

Your "big one" is your gift.

Writers write.

Singers sing.

Dancers dance.

You're a hedgehog now, not a fox.

You're a Master-of-One now, not a Jack-of-All-Trades.

Stick to your "big one" because it's your gift; to you and from you to the world.

Gold in the Dirt

I had a sales coach once. He was big on cold-calling, which is analogous to sifting for gold. This sales coach had a saying: "I'm not trying to turn the dirt into gold; I'm trying to find the gold in the dirt."

When I sold life insurance, I'd make three hundred cold-calls a day all for one sale, two if I was lucky. Using what my sales coach taught me, here's how a typical call went:

RING! RING! RING!

"Hello?"

"This Marty?"

"Yeah this is Marty."

"Great. Listen. Reason for the call today: saw you filled out a form for life insurance—lemme ask you, were you looking to leave a little something behind for your family, or just enough to cover basic burial expenses?"

If the prospect's answer wasn't one of the two choices provided, I hung up.

Why? Why not try and convince him he needed life insurance? Why not try and get him to see the logic behind his potential buying decision?

Because I wasn't trying to turn the dirt into gold; I was trying to find the gold in the dirt.

A similar thing happens when you achieve self-mastery. After years of sifting through the soot of success, you find the gold in the dirt—your gift.

Fly—Part One

I had a meeting over coffee with my friend David one morning.

"How are you?" David said, crossing one leg over the other. Before I could answer, he continued: "Better yet, how are you feeling?"

Just days removed from completing my hero's journey, I smiled and said: "Anxious. Not in the sense of being fearful of the future, but in the sense of anticipation. I'm wondering what's next? I'm ready to go."

David leaned back in his wooden chair. "My youngest loves bugs right now," he said. "He's all about 'em. Last weekend, my stepdad came over and dropped off a butterfly kit for him."

I chuckled. The nostalgia from having a butterfly kit myself at that age cracked a smile on my face.

"This weekend, the caterpillars came in the mail. He and I got the whole thing set up. We put the caterpillars inside, the whole nine. Then my youngest [son] claps his hands and says, 'When do they become butterflies?'"

I chuckled again.

Kids, man.

"I told him it usually takes a couple weeks at least," David said. "I share that story with you, Hunter, because most people think the hardest part of the caterpillar turning into the butterfly is the waiting period when it's inside the cocoon." David's mouth went flat like a lipless wound. He shook his head. "It's not the waiting part that's the hardest. It's when the butterfly breaks out of the cocoon—he has to use muscles he doesn't know he has to do something he doesn't even know how to do. But he takes off anyway."

I nodded my acknowledgment.

"God's getting you ready for something, Hunter. And when the time is right, you're gonna fly."

Same goes for you.

After achieving self-mastery, there may be an anxious anticipation for "what's next?" that may require patience.

But when the time comes for you to fly, God may ask you to use muscles you didn't know you had; to do something you didn't know you could do—like become a Table Topics Champion.

You're not a Lifelong Caterpillar, you're supposed to change. And when the time comes for you to break out of your cocoon, like the butterfly, you will need to take off anyway.

Don't worry.

You're gonna fly.

Fly—Part Two

One morning, our cat Clarence—we have three in all, they're the best—was meowing to be let outside just as I set down my eggs at the kitchen table.

"Yeah, yeah," I said. "I hear ya, buddy."

I barely got the sliding door open before Clarence leapt outside—right onto a finch.

The poor bird went limp in Clarence's maw like a spineless doll. Clarence brought it inside and dropped him near my feet. "Here, dad," is what I imagine he would have said if he could talk. "And you were about to eat eggs?"

The finch flapped its wings, then hopped up to its feet.

A second later, it took off. Clarence must have done some damage, because the finch flew in a drunken circle before drilling the sliding glass door.

When it did, it fell like a cinder block.

Clarence pounced on the bird again in a flash, clamping his jaws around its neck and bringing it to the welcome mat at our front door.

I was certain it was dead.

After a few moments, the finch gathered itself, hopping up to its feet again but stayed grounded this time. The way it staggered back and forth reminded me of my dad suffering that stroke on the basketball court.

I put myself between the finch and Clarence. "You're okay," I said, cupping the bird in my hand. "You're okay." I was expecting it to flail about, or peck at my fingers. It didn't resist me at all. There was a stillness to it that felt like trust.

A trust that resembled faith.

I walked onto the back porch, opening my hands slowly, saying: "You're okay."

The bird looked back at me with its beady little eyes, blinking twice.

"You're okay," I said, nodding back. "More than okay."

The little finch turned its sights to the skies, flapped its wings and flew away.

What an amazing allegory to the way God works in our lives, wouldn't you agree?

Though things may look bleak at times, we must never forget who is with us. Even if we're in dire straits like my finch friend, we must trust when all else fails. When we've reached the end of ourselves, that's when faith begins—the faith to fly when we're not sure we can; the faith to use muscles we didn't know we had; the guts to go all-in on the gift He gave us.

That's self-mastery.

Be All You Can Be—Part One

“Be all you can be,” was the best advice Mr. Peña ever gave me.

Let that simmer for a moment.

The Trillion Dollar Man who, as far as I know, has all the stuff one could want—and then some. Keeping that in mind, Mr. Peña didn’t tell me to “have all you can have” or “do all you can do.”

Mr. Peña said: “Be all you can be.”

Life isn’t about having more.

Life isn’t about doing more.

Life is about being more.

You’re not a human *having*.

You’re not a human *doing*.

You’re a human *being*.

Be all you can be.

Be All You Can Be—Part Two

"You can be anything you want," is what most parents tell their children.

That's nice, but I think it's a load of crap.

Let's face it, the world isn't a buffet; you don't have unlimited choices.

There's only one option: being all you *can* be. Meaning, whatever gift God has given you is your destiny. It's your assignment.

And here's the thing: you don't know the upper limit of being all you *can* be, or if there is one.

If you were born to write, then it's your moral obligation to be the best writer you can be; you don't get to be a professional athlete and an entrepreneurial mastermind and expect to become a *New York Times Bestselling* author.

Believe me, I've tried. It doesn't work.

You're only one person.

You can't be anything you want; you don't have unlimited choices.

But you can be all you *can* be.

Be All You Can Be—Part Three

Speaking of bestselling authors, Bob Goff, whom I'm a great admirer of, quits one thing every week. Bob knows what he's supposed to be doing—telling stories. That's Bob's one big trick, he's a hedgehog. If something he's adopted slows him down, or takes him away from his gift, he quits it.

Not long after Mr. Peña's resignation, I had to look myself in the mirror and admitted I did not have the bandwidth to stay on as President of Kiwanis, a member of the Grand Rapids Rotary Club, and Toastmasters Table Topics champ—they had tapped me to be our club's president for the next year.

I decided to step away from all three organizations.

I was becoming a *human doing*.

It would have led to a disservice to the organizations and what's more, it was becoming a form of self-sabotage; slowing me down on finishing this book.

It's okay to walk away from one arena if it helps you run in another.

The steepest hill may be the hardest to run up, but it's also the one that will slow you down the most.

Bob Goff is no dummy.

Be like Bob, quit something this week because you've got work to do—and only a finite time to do it.

Be all you *can* be, or you may never be all you *can.*

Be All You Can Be—Part Four

My favorite verse in the Bible comes from the Gospel of John 1:14: "The Word became flesh and made His dwelling among us." What that verse means is, God became a human being in the form of His son, Jesus Christ, and walked with us for thirty-three years.

I think something similar happens when we stop trying so hard when it comes to writing our book, producing our screenplay, or composing our symphony. I call it, *letting God hijack you.* Meaning, you and I no longer have instruments.

The writer's fingers aren't his.

The singer's voice isn't hers.

The entrepreneur's vision doesn't belong to him.

When we let God hijack us, completely letting go and creating "whatever comes to us" we no longer have an instrument. We become the instrument—His instrument.

We're no longer playing God with each work we produce.

We're letting God play us—and the Word becomes flesh and makes His dwelling among us—producing works in this world, but not of it.

That's being all you can be.

Empathy and Connection—Part One

Paul Rink once told Steven Pressfield: "Suffering never hurt any writer that I know of."

In my opinion, that's a euphemism for a saying of mine: *where empathy flows, connection grows.*

Take Pressfield and Stephen King for example. The former didn't have his first book published until he was *fifty-four* years old, and if you've read any of Pressfield's books, you know there was a great deal of suffering in the decades leading up to that first book deal. King, on the other hand, wrote the all-time great vampire novel, *Salem's Lot,* in the little spare time he had when he wasn't working at the laundromat. As for me, there were many nights spent in the broom closet at Subway writing the book you're holding.

The three of us, and I'm no literary giant like Pressfield or King, had a rough go at this thing. We suffered. But in hindsight, was it really suffering? I don't think so. What an outlet for content creation, right? Making sandwiches can be seen as an art—the position is called *Sandwich Artist,* after all—which lends itself to new concepts and perspectives. And some of the stories you hear from customers? C'mon. It's stealing. All the stuff we see on a daily basis builds a bridge from us to our audience because we know where they're at. Where empathy flows, connection grows.

Rink was right.

Suffering didn't hurt this writer.
Suffering won't hurt you either.
Not one bit.

Empathy and Connection—Part Two

This goes without saying, but just so we're clear, Rink's axiom isn't exclusive to writers. Everyone suffers, and the majority suffer a great deal more, and for far longer than our crooked politicians, corrupt government officials, and the gajillionaires running the world.

If that's the case, and it is, why do so many people try to pander to those at the top of the proverbial hierarchy rather than the bottom?

Golden Calves.

Said another way, aspiring authors, songwriters, personal development coaches and the like are literally marketing to, or trying to emulate themselves as, the top *one percent* of the population.

I don't mean to sound crass, but that's a bad strategy.

I'm not saying we ought to be success-seeking with our gift in search of the Almighty Dollar (we've already been down that road, haven't we?). What I'm saying is that if we want our book, our album, our art collection to get into as many hands as possible, then why are we marketing to the fewest hands possible—those at the top?

If you want your gift to be shared with the world, then you've got to embrace Rink's advice. You need to be okay with suffering, because the majority of the world's population is doing just that—suffering. When they read, see, and know that you feel their pain, connection is inevitable.

Where empathy flows, connection grows.

The reverse is also true.

I see so many guys and gals spending thousands of dollars on high quality video production peddling this, that, and the other. Yet they wonder why their work isn't selling.

The answer is simple.

They haven't suffered enough. Those who have suffered considerably—their audience—see right through it. Their pitch is too perfect, too rehearsed, too grandiose. As a result, their message doesn't align with the audience's lives because they haven't endured their own Road of Trials, so to speak.

Where empathy flows, connection grows.

A Different Game—Part One

Odds are, the next hero's journey you take—or the one you're currently on, which I'm honored to be part of by extension of this book—won't be your last.

While writing this book, I went on two more hero's journeys back-to-back.

Each one was shorter and more intense than the last.

The hero's journey in part two lasted 308 days. The next, which will serve as the sequel to this book, was less than half as long at 146 days.

The one after that? *Forty-two* days.

Why was each subsequent journey so much shorter?

I had the map.

I wasn't able to predict exactly which stage of the journey I was on, nor the next stage to come. But like playing football, there was play recognition; I could see what was happening as it was unfolding. I knew I was on a hero's journey.

I became hyper-aware that I needed to be learning something.

A part of me needed to die—another head of Default's Hydra needed to be slain.

I was undergoing another transformation.

I was vigilant in every aspect of my life.

And since you have the map now, you will be too.

With each hero's journey you will undergo, as I did, a sort of circumambulation, or upward spiral into the person God created you to be.

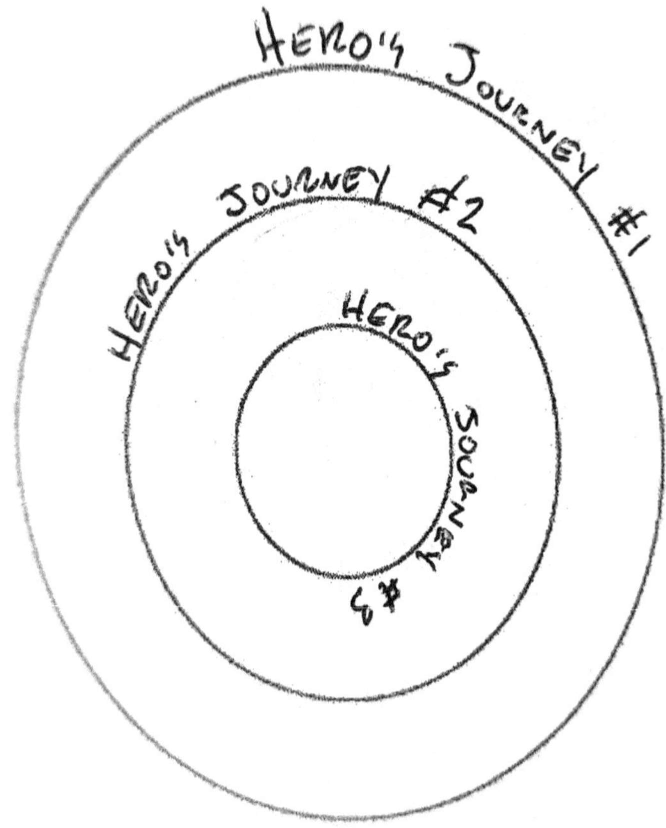

Image 10: Concentric circles representing successive hero's journey's; each one being briefer than before. The outermost circle being the biggest and longest to complete, the innermost being the briefest. Source: Hunter M. Charneski

What happens when you reach the end—your final hero's journey?

Well, then you can finally, after all these years, scratch your own itch.

You can go off the script.

You're playing a different game now.

A Different Game—Part Two

Once you see your life through the lens of a story that is the hero's journey, a few things happen:

- Each hero's journey becomes your next *Gift for the People* in the form of the next book, collection, or business idea.
- You're more patient, less judgmental. You recognize when others are on their own hero's journey, or aren't meant to be part of yours. Because of that, your—get this—*Default,* is giving them grace instead of holding a grudge.
- You start living more adventurously, like a playful child. When tough decisions present themselves, you don't ask: "What should I do?" but instead: "What would make for a better story?"

You're playing a different game now.

Self-Mastery and Fear

When I was selling life insurance, I made an old-fashioned house call on a Friday night, visiting my friend Chris in Detroit.

Chris is an entrepreneur in the telecommunications industry.

Chris' business is valued well over $10M.

Chris didn't have a single cent of life insurance.

Why didn't Chris have any life insurance coverage?

He had an irrational fear of doctors, kind of like kids are scared that sharks might be in swimming pools.

"I know this is something I need to do, and this process is going to make me do it," Chris said in the leather chair across from me. We were smoking stogies in his cigar room. He pistoned an arm out to the ashtray on the coffee table between us, flicked the delicate tube of ash off the end of his Montecristo, then continued: "I'm just scared to death to go to the doctor."

"I understand," I said, staring down the brown barrel of my own cigar. The orangish-red tip produced lazy tendrils of smoke climbing slowly toward the ceiling vent. "But lemme ask you a question."

"Go ahead," Chris said.

I shrugged, plucked the cigar from my mouth and said: "Have you ever thought going to the doctor might be a good thing?"

Crows' feet formed at the corner of Chris' eyes. "How

do you mean?"

"Before I left this afternoon," I said, crossing one leg over the other. "I usually go out the front door because Tiffany and Sam are home. But since they're in Cincinnati, I locked it and went out the garage." I leaned forward, talking with my hands. "Now, we usually keep the door leading to the garage in the breezeway open because our cats like hanging out in there."

"Yeah," Chris said, the cigar bobbing between his lips.

"Here's the thing about our cats, especially Clarence, they would do anything to be outside. In fact, if Clarence got out?" I made a *pssh!* sound. "We ain't ever seeing him again. So, I go out into the garage and Clarence is napping in the corner by the studs and pink insulation. Now, whenever we open the garage door, it scares the crap out of him and he sprints inside the house."

Chris nodded his acknowledgment.

"Why am I telling you this?" I asked, leaning toward him. "Because if Clarence faced his fear and ran toward the garage door instead of away from it, he would literally have the one thing he wants more than anything—he'd be outside."

In sterquiliniis invenitur.

Chris' eyes went glassy like a doll's. "Wow," he said.

"Moral of the story?" I said, then parked the cigar between my lips. "Don't be like my cat. Run toward your fear. Everything you want is on the other side of it. Fear is the signal for you to do the thing."

That's self-mastery.

SECTION II: OFF THE SCRIPT

Off the Script—Part One

A few weeks before opening my gym, I attended a seminar held at the home of then Carolina Panthers' head strength coach.

Of all the concepts that made up his training philosophy—and there were plenty—one stood out to me amongst the rest. Something he called, *Off the Script,* or OTS for short.

The idea of OTS is simple: when the plan a coach had in mind for the day's training session with his athletes isn't going well, change it. Don't wait. Do it then and there. There's no need to see a bad workout through to the end just because he spent an hour writing it.

Not going *off the script* would be doing himself and, more importantly, his athletes a huge disservice.

This is hypothetical, but not really—you'd be shocked how many coaches don't go off the script, even when it's glaringly obvious they need to—let's imagine a coach's plan for the day includes a one-rep max on deadlift. His clientele consists primarily of high school athletes—and they just had prom the night before. They're tired. They're groggy. They have a general malaise toward life itself that day. They can hardly bend over, much less *max out* on a deadlift. But the coach doesn't give a rip because that's the plan for today's session and he's sticking to it.

Stupid.

That's like self-sabotage on steroids.

You see where this is going?

A Self-Sabotaging Man loves to stick to the plan, no matter how badly it's going. A man who's achieved self-mastery knows he doesn't need to see this life through just because he's spent decades living it. A Self-Sabotaging Man knows he needs to stop chasing Golden Calves. A man who's achieved self-mastery knows better; he walks away, no matter how much time, money, and effort he's invested.

A man who's achieved self-mastery knows he can't rewrite what's already been written.

A man who's achieved self-mastery makes a change then and there.

He starts a new chapter.

He goes *off the script.*

Off the Script—Part Two

In that same coffee meeting with my friend David, we debriefed after I had given a keynote speech to a group of men and women at Mel Trotter Ministries (at the time, David served as Head of the Workforce Development Program at MTM).

"I thought your speech was fantastic," David said. "But here's something to consider. I don't care if a speaker gets through every single slide of his PowerPoint. I care about connection, which you do a great job of, but I wonder if you could connect even more without a PowerPoint?"

"What do you mean?" I asked.

"What do you think would happen if you went *off the script?"*

I couldn't believe he said that, either.

I fluttered my lips. "You mean give a ninety-minute keynote extemporaneously?"

A two-minute Table Topics speech is one thing—but an hour-and-a-half? C'mon.

"You know what you're trying to communicate," David said, lines forming on his forehead. "I can tell you know it well. I'd encourage you to go off the script when we see you again next week. You can do it."

David was right. I know what I was trying to communicate. It's my story.

Do you need a script to communicate what you already know?

Did Beethoven need to hear music in order to compose

it?

Does Stephen King try to know what happens in the next horror scene he writes, or does it just bleed out of him?

Did Lil Wayne need a script for perhaps the most famous hip-hop lyric of all-time: "Feed me rappers or feed me beats"?

Or did they, like those who go all-in on their gift, know what they're trying to communicate so well, they were able to go *off the script?*

You know what you're trying to communicate. It's your story.

Go off the script.

See what happens.

Here's How it Works

As I mentioned earlier, I used to do some copywriting.

I wasn't great, but I was good enough to get by. Reason being, I was clear, not clever or cute. After hooking the prospect by sharing a brief story to gain his empathy and trust as his guide, I had to be as clear as possible when laying out the plan. When it came to the plan, I simply wrote: *Here's how it works.*

With that in mind, the next few chapters are going to hit you right between the eyes on the three steps I used to stop self-sabotage and achieve self-mastery. They're going to help you go off the script and start that new chapter.

Be warned. It might feel rudimentary.

It might leave you frowning, thinking: *really, that's it?*

These steps aren't here to entertain you.

They're here to help you.

Speaking of help, I'm not a self-help guru. But I do know in order to execute a plan, two things are needed: simplicity and transparency.

No weird alliteration.

No freaky-deaky rhymes.

No sales pitch.

I'm just going to give it to you straight.

So, here's how it works….

Put God First—Part Three

Make God the priority in your life.

I could end the chapter right there. Unfortunately, we've bastardized the word *priority* for over one hundred years. Most people don't even understand what the word *priority* means.

Greg McKeown explains in his bestselling book, *Essentialism:*

> *The word priority came into the English language in the 1400s. It was singular. It meant the very first or prior thing. It stayed singular for the next five hundred years.*
>
> *Only in the 1900s did we pluralize the term and start talking about priorities. Illogically, we reasoned that by changing the word we could bend reality. Somehow, we would now be able to have multiple 'first' things.*
>
> *People and companies routinely try to do just that. One leader told me of this experience in a company that talked of 'Pri-1, Pri-2, Pri-3, Pri-4, and Pri-5.' This gave the impression of many things being the priority but actually meant nothing*

was.

Make God the (one and only) priority in your life.

God comes before your job.

God comes before your family.

God comes before your gift.

Why?

He gave you all those things—and Part One showed He can definitely take it all away.

How do you put God first?

Here's what I do: I put God first by reading my Bible first thing in the morning, every morning.[41]

I might read a chapter.

I might read an entire book.

I might read a single verse.

I read until something leaps off the page and grabs my attention. From there, I open my journal and write that verse, or passage down, verbatim. Then I write, just as Mrs. Schmitz said, whatever comes to me as it relates to that particular passage or verse.

If the verse is about humility, I write to God, asking Him to keep me humble.

If the verse is about the danger of passing judgment, I write to God that He may keep me from said danger.

If the verse is about mercy, I write about how merciful He's been to me, and how I hope and pray He'll continue to show mercy.

It's not journaling or free-writing, per se. It's more like refined prayer.

This goes on for a page, typically. Lastly—and this is

---

[41] Where should you begin? I could punt and say anywhere, but if I were you, I'd start with the Gospel of Mark. It's the shortest and most chronologically correct of the Gospels. And Mark, like myself, hits you right between the eyes as he invites you into the story of his walk with Jesus.

important—after glancing at the passage and prayer, I say out loud: "What do you want me to do Lord, in response to this passage and prayer?" The answer usually comes to me as I'm asking the question, sometimes before.

"Be still."

"Have more faith."

"Listen."

The words float into my mind's eye like the bottom of a Magic Eight Ball. And when they do, I write them down.

Fast-forward twenty-four hours.

After a full day of busyness, solving problems at Subway, and just the general, everyday happenings of life, I don't remember much of what I wrote the day before, if anything. But when I crack open my journal, I review yesterday's passage, prayer, and instruction, it's eerie. I saw how much I needed that particular passage; it was the prompt for the prayer I wrote which was a preview for the life I lived the day before because I did what He told me to do— "Be still…Have more faith…Listen…" It's dictation, divine inspiration, all of that.

But what's more, I'm getting to know Him. And the more I get to know Him, the more I realize He truly is the Author of my life; all I have to do is read what I wrote the day before—because it happened. If it didn't happen that day, it typically does in the coming days or weeks. And when it does, I remember what I wrote, as well as everything that led up to it; it's like a miniature Epiphanal Moment inside a truncated hero's journey.

It's cool.

When you realize He is the Author of your life and that He is gracious enough to share that power with you, the power to change your story, you won't waste time in making Him the priority in your life.

And if you don't put God first, I can't speak for Mr. Jones, but you might just lose everything.

Go All-In—Part Three

Going all-in will be hard.

When it gets hard, you'd be wise to remember Paul Rink's quote about suffering never hurting any writer—or whatever gift you possess—he knew of. You'd be *really* wise to remember Leslie Chow's quote in the motion picture *The Hangover.*

"But did you die?"

It's funny, yes, but that quote will bring tremendous levity when you're wondering what the hell you're doing on Day 371[42] of going all-in. If you're anything like me, don't be surprised if this is how it all goes down when you go all-in on your gift:

- When you burn the Golden Calf(s) in your life and Put God first, you become spiritually reborn (i.e., you're no longer an overgrown infant, but a spiritual one).
- Can newborns eat solid food? Of course not. They can only drink milk. I'm going to sound contradictory to what I said in the chapter titled: *Default and Going All-In*, but there's a time for everything. Keeping that in mind, there may be a

[42] At the time this chapter was written, the date was May 16, 2024—371 days after completing the hero's journey Part Two comprises—and trust me, going all-in has been hard.

period of time—for me it was six months, from March to September, 2023—where the only thing God will want you to do is write your book, paint your collection, or record your album. This bears repeating: **the only thing God will want you to do is** go all-in on your gift.

- In the meantime, you might go into debt. Your cell service might be disconnected. Your wife, son, and in-laws may emasculate you because you're not doing anything but the work you've been running away from your entire life.

"But did you die?"

As a newborn in Christ, it'll be hard getting used to Him meeting your needs, not your *wants,* but your needs. He will help you grow in front of your wife, son, and in-laws, into the man He created you to be. He'll help you get your house in order. You'll be just a baby—fully reliant on Him. As paradoxical as it sounds, that's how a Man of God becomes a man, in my opinion. Only after you've learned what you need to, which may include going on another hero's journey, or two, will He provide some solid food, like a job, to build you back up. Don't expect it to be glorious, even if your resume looks like mine. Heck, you might start out as a Sandwich Artist at Subway.

But a job is better than no job, lemme tell you.

Once you've proven to Him, and to everyone else for that matter, that you're no longer going to sacrifice your gift to another Golden Calf, that's when—and I'm only speaking from firsthand experience, here—you'll earn His favor. You know, the kind of favor you felt robbed of in your childhood? Yeah, that kind of favor as a man who goes all-in might look like:

- You'll land a job that fits your schedule perfectly, allowing you ample time to cultivate your gift and contribute to the bottom line without robbing you of quality time with loved ones.

- Your spouse or partner will get a raise; a new job; some crazy, unheard of bonus that shouldn't have happened, but did, in order to meet your needs.
- Opportunities seemingly orient themselves toward you; people will present chances for you to share your gift to gain experience and confidence and real-world validation.
- He'll elevate you at Subway or Burger King or Taco-Bell, promoting you to Manager, then Multi-Unit Manager, then District Manager in less than nine-months' time—again, I'm speaking from experience.

That's a good deal—if you're willing to stick it out.
"But did you die?"
Go all-in.

Run *Your* Race—Part Three

Friend and coach, Tony Holler, once told me: "Speed grows like a tree."

Same goes for your gift.

Since that's the case, you may be inclined to rip out your gift before it takes root; to slash it as a sapling; to not put enough care and effort into it so it can stand the test of time.

Why?

Think back to my last indoor meet in Part Two, the one where I set a new personal record but came in third instead of winning.

We compete against others who share a similar gift.

We race someone else instead of running *our* race.

We let our old Default creep back in with victim-like questions in our head:

- *"When am I gonna get mine?"*
- *"Why can't I just catch a break?"*
- *"I shouldn't have to keep doing this stupid job when the real work is (INSERT YOUR GIFT HERE)."*

When those questions come up, and they will, remind yourself that you're not a victim.

And who said it was about you, anyways?

Your gift was never yours to begin with—God gave it to you so you could give it to other Self-Sabotaging Men under the dominion of Default.

It's your moral obligation to help them fail to fulfill their Default's obligation, and then redefine their Default, creating new obligations to fulfill, better, healthier ones.

And here's another paradox: realize that the process really is greater than the product.

The feel-good moment from completing a project is fleeting.

But working toward the completion of a project? Whoa. That's way better—better than sex, even—and the *feel good* isn't a moment, it's momentum.

As a sprinter, it pains me to say this, but your race might be a marathon. If your novel, symphony, or start-up is "taking forever," consider yourself in good company.

- J.K. Rowling took six years to finish *Harry Potter and the Sorcerer's Stone.*
- *Beethoven's Fifth* took him as many years to complete.
- For their first eight years in business, *Nike* was (hardly) known as *Blue Ribbon Sports.*

How do you run *your* race? I don't know. Everyone's different. You're going to have to "train" through hundreds of hours of trial and error to figure out what your pace is.

As a writer, I can only offer suggestions specific to the craft. I used to think 1,000 words a day was the goal, come hell or high water. Meh. Not anymore. A word count made me neurotic. A daily requirement made me tyrannical. No, I don't write everyday, but most days I do.

Same goes for sprinting.

No, I don't have a set word count, I just act like a regular person and write until I have to go to work. I write more on the weekends because I have more time.

Same goes for sprinting.

I write more when I'm really feeling it. I write less when I'm not. I don't write if something comes up, like my family or wife or something unforeseen.

Same goes for sprint—you get the gist.

Okay I lied. One last note about sprinting. I can say that being too rigid with my training has always, at best, led to crappy workouts and at worse, led to injuries.

Same goes for your gift.

If you're feeling great, then get after it.

If you're feeling like crap, back off or don't even do it.

Leave yourself in a good place with your gift every day, and running your race will be a *want to,* not a *have to.*

> *"The horse who loves to run beats the horse who feels compelled to every single time." – Steven Pressfield, Turning Pro*

Your gift grows like a tree.

It'll take twice as long as you think, so start yesterday.

Don't compare yourself to others.

Find the pace that works best for you.

And when you do, there's no competition.

Run *your* race.

Gravity

Here's the thing about self-mastery: you will inevitably feel regret; regret from all those years you wasted sabotaging yourself.

I've been there, which is why I want you to consider the following scene from my wife's and my favorite movie, *Interstellar.* In this particular scene, Cooper (played by Matthew McConaughey) and Dr. Brand (played by Anne Hathaway) have royally screwed up. They were investigating a planet outside our galaxy to see if it had natural resources (oxygen, water, etc.) to sustain life for the human race because earth was just about kaput—and earth only had enough food for two more generations, tops. But the planet they investigated had one downside: time sped up in a major way—one hour there was equal to *seven years* on earth. Long story short, their investigation ends disastrously. Their ship breaks down, leaving them stranded on the planet for hours….losing more than twenty-three years back on earth.

Here's how that scene unfolds.

> "Is there any possibility, I don't know, some kinda way we could maybe, I don't know, jump in a black hole—gain back the years?" Cooper said, panting.
>
> Brand shakes her head.
>
> "Don't shake your head at me."
>
> "Time is relative, okay?" Brand

> said, nodding and catching her breath. "It can stretch, and it can squeeze, but," she shakes her head again. "*It can't run backwards.* It can't. The only thing that can move across dimensions, like *time,* is gravity."
>
> "Okay," Cooper says, wagging a finger at Brand. "The Beings that led us here…They communicate through gravity, right?" He says, wringing his hands together.
>
> Brand nods, visibly defeated. "Yep."
>
> "Could They be talking to us from the future?"
>
> "Maybe."
>
> "*They can.*"
>
> "They…" Brand cranes her neck forward, whispering. "*They* are beings of five dimensions. To them, time might be another physical dimension. To them, the past might be a canyon they can crawl down into and the future: a mountain they can climb up, but to us it's *not,* okay?"

Who's They? You might be wondering, but I think you already know.

(Look up)

Fast forward to the *Deus Ex Machina* scene: Cooper jumps into a black hole, goes back in time vis-a-vis gravity and establishes contact with his daughter, Murph. Cooper shares his discovery with his daughter—that time can be rearranged with gravity. Murph takes that discovery and saves the human race from extinction.

Hey-o!

June 16, 2023

My wife and I were in our living room discussing the book you're holding.

"The manuscript is finished," I said. "But I don't have an editor, much less an agent, and it could take months of query letters for the latter. And up to a year after that for a publisher to get back to us. What I'm trying to say is that we might not see a dime of revenue from this book for a year, at least."

What happened three hours later makes me believe God must've been listening.

"A year?" I imagine He said, slapping His knee in a fit of laughter. "Hey Gabriel," He said, waving the archangel over. "Get a load of this! Dude said: 'a year, at least'," God handed Gabriel a chalice. "Here, hold my wine...."

A California number came up on my phone.

"Hello?" I answered sheepishly.

"Hello Hunter, my name is Sharon and I'm a literary agent. I just received your intro from a friend and I'd like to talk to you about your book."

I signed with Sharon ten days later.

As for my editor, David? Maybe a day after that.

Don't be surprised when things in your life happen at warp speed when you finally go off the script, defeating your Default. I believe that with every fiber of my being. How couldn't I? I lived it.

All those years were not wasted. God's just rearranging them, using His love and the *gravity* of your situation to pull it all back to the here and now.

SECTION III: SCRATCH YOUR OWN ITCH

Scratch Your Own Itch—Part One

Scratch Your Own Itch is a concept I've used for several years as a piece of advice.

I think it's self-explanatory, but I'll explain anyway.

If you're wired for entrepreneurship, but you're not sure what to do or what to offer the marketplace, I would tell you to scratch your own itch, not someone else's.

Sure, it's easier to fill a demand than create a demand. I get that. But it's easier to fill your demand than someone else's. If you're filling someone else's demand instead of your own, you will need to create the demand for yourself first.

That's not scratching your own itch.

That's propagandistic at best and self-sabotage at worst; all that nonsense is behind you now.

You're not going back to what you know.

Step into the unknown.

You have an itch, are you scratching it?

Let It Go

Everyone has that brother, mother-in-law, friend, or cousin who holds a gift over your head long after they've given it to you; especially when you've got better things to do than engaging in self-sabotaging activities with them like you used to.

"Well," they'll scoff, placing a hand on either hip. "I gave you a refrigerator (or a car, a loan, a laptop, etc.) didn't I? Going to the bar with me is the least you could do."

Here's the thing. It was never a gift if they're still holding onto it.

Same thing goes for *your* gift.

If you never ship your manuscript to the publisher, pitch your business plan to investors, fundraise for new research that will cure cancer, then it's not a gift. There's going to come a time when you're going to have to let go, man.

In order for it to be a gift, it has to be given, and you can't hold onto it.

God gave it to you so you could give it to the world.

Ship it.

Pitch it.

Let it go.

Done > Perfect

And when you let it go, you've got to reconcile with the fact that it's not going to be perfect.

This book isn't perfect, far from it, and it never will be.

But it's done, isn't it?

Done is better than perfect.

How to Finish—Part One

Get serious, first and foremost.

Get intentional about your gift becoming your full-time gig.

Surround yourself with individuals whose job is to pitch your project. Get an agent. Build a Dream Team. They're going to give you a deadline, and you're going to stick to it.

When it comes time for you to ship it, it might not be perfect, but it will be done.

You can't hold onto it.

You've got to let it go.

That's how you finish.

How to Finish—Part Two

Start the next project before the current WIP, (Work In Progress) is done. The excitement of starting something new will make the WIP feel like it's a job—and that's kind of the point, isn't it? Your gift becoming your full-time gig?—which will expedite its completion so you can focus on the next project.

That's how you finish.

Paying It Backward—Part Two

An update on my friend and former Director of Operations of my gym, Thomas.

He took that gym and made it his own—in every way.

When I was the owner, we trained middle school girl soccer players.

When he was the owner, their focus was on high school baseball players.

I operated out of a small commercial suite i.e., a garage.

Within a year, he had to move to a warehouse—quintupling the gym's size and client roster.

My gym was called *Freak Faktory Barbell & Sports Performance.*

His gym was called *Optimal Performance.*

After owning it for over three years, I gave it to Thomas.

After Thomas owned it for over three years, Thomas gave it to his brother so he could pursue a new career in—check this out—the financial industry. Isn't that rich?

When I gave my gym to Thomas, I wasn't paying it forward. I dumped it on his lap so I could jettison to the other side of the country. I was paying it backward. Giving that gym away was the most selfish thing I've ever done.

When Thomas gave his gym to his brother, he *was* paying it forward. He didn't expect anything in return. He didn't leave Michigan. He still lives right down the road from the gym. I can't speak for Thomas, but I reckon giving that gym away was one of the most selfless things he's ever done.

Thomas learned from my mistake. He knew if he was going to give that gym away, he was going to do it the right way.[43] Thomas scratched his own itch.

---

[43] Thomas' brother still runs the gym, and it's thriving.

Artistic Warriors—Part One

I think there's a large group of men who've been orphaned in the personal development space—I call them *Artistic Warriors.*

These guys are those creative alpha males who enjoy building their bodies like Michelangelo's *God and Adam* as much as they do painting it.

They have strong work ethics and a child-like sense of play.

These dudes aren't afraid to lace up their boots and get after it, and they're not ashamed to kick their feet up after a long day on the job and play *Destiny* on Xbox.

These men are writers, singers, entrepreneurs, painters, and the like.

They're also athletes, bodybuilders, and health nuts.

The only problem is, what tribe, or group, exists for them?

To the best of my knowledge, there isn't one. Most personal development gurus and performance coaches I've listened to are either on one end of the spectrum, macho and money-focused, or the other, artsy fartsy or hyper-philosophical, with a gap between the two—a gaping wound that's bleeding out the potential integration of both alpha and artist.

It's no wonder why Artistic Warriors feel orphaned—because they are. And I think, though I have no way of proving this, some Artistic Warriors never have their *After the Wilderness* Epiphanal Moment like Steven Pressfield's

Writing Wednesday email. They're doomed to Default and slaves to self-sabotage for the rest of their lives.

As bad as that sounds, the good news is the reverse is also true.

If those guys find their tribe—and I'm biased of course—I don't think there's a more ready and willing man to help today's Self-Sabotaging Man than the Artistic Warrior.

They've stared into the abyss.

They know the darkness all too well, which makes the dark scared of them, not the other way around.

They're strong and silver-tongued.

They're intense and intelligent.

They're creative and conscientious.

They can make money—and move mountains.

They can build things.

They can break things.

They see things differently, which is why they make great CEOs.

They're orphans who've made it out of the wilderness.

They're Artistic Warriors, and they know The Way out of self-sabotage and into self-mastery.

Artistic Warriors—Part Two

There's a shift that happens when a Self-Sabotaging Man achieves self-mastery.

For him, it's no longer about impressing people. It's about impressing upon other Self-Sabotaging Men the goodness of the gift God's given him.

My hope is—and as Mr. Peña would say, "hope isn't a strategy"—the more time other Self-Sabotaging Men spend with him, they'll start asking questions.

They want whatever he's got.

They want a fraction of the action.

They want a piece for their niece.

They want a tad for Brad.

You feel me? I've always wanted to say that.

What if all men who've achieved self-mastery—and that includes you now—used their God-given gift to help Self-Sabotaging Men go all in on theirs?

Better question: what if all Self-Sabotaging Men achieved self-mastery?

They'd become Artistic Warriors. I don't know about you, but a world without Self-Sabotaging Men sounds like heaven on earth.

I don't think I'm overstating this: it only takes one person to create a massive ripple effect, and it doesn't take much effort either—like a leaf falling on the lake's still surface.

Are you that one person?

Are you the outlier that will save civilization?

I sure hope so. God knows we need you now more than ever. You know The Way out of self-sabotage. Don't keep it to yourself. Help other Self-Sabotaging Men make the transformation you have. It's your new obligation; your new Default.

A Worthy Investment—Part Two

You're worth it.

Read that again.

It doesn't matter if you've fallen away from God and the gift He's given you.

It doesn't matter if you've lost touch with Him—even if it's been years.

It doesn't matter.

He will always be there no matter what, and He'll be overjoyed to hear from you.

How do I know?

Bill and Kyle Galik. Do you remember them?

Bill was like a dad to me. Kyle was my best friend.

Then, seven years went by. Default had me in its death-grip. I fell away from both of them, not calling either once—not even sending a text.

In the summer of 2022, I called on both of them; not to genuinely reconnect, but to see if they'd be interested in buying life insurance. Kyle bought a policy. Bill went on to lend me $31K to attend QLA—money he wasn't interested in seeing a return on, at that.

They treated me as if not a day had gone by.

Bananas.

Bill and Kyle's unconditional love is analogous to God the Father and Jesus' love for you. Yes, *you.*

They'll always be there, no matter what.

They'll be willing to, as Bill did, invest in you—because you're worth it.

Read that again.

A New Default—Part Two

Redefining Default won't be easy—it's the story you've been telling yourself for as long as you can remember.

But when you change your story, does that mean you change, or redefine your Default as well?

Consider Dr. Jordan B. Peterson's reflection on his first in-person viewing of Michelangelo's *David.* He was intimidated, as he should have been. A piece of art like that would make anyone feel like they weren't nearly what they could be, and with good reason.

Are you a General Manager at Subway when you know darn well you've got the chops to be a District Manager, but are intimidated by the responsibility that comes with a job like that; or who you might have to become?

Can you throw a baseball ninety-five miles per hour, but if you got disciplined with your diet, had a stellar sleep schedule, and cut out all the Lifelong Caterpillars from your life, how likely would 100 miles per hour become a reality?

Is the song you sing in the shower the next big hit that'll put Taylor Swift to shame and bring you to fame? But doing so requires you get out of the bathroom and onto the stage; out of your birthday suit and into your costume? Strange times are these when we'd rather be naked than noteworthy.

Michelangelo's *David* is one of art history's masterpieces. An argument could be made that no other artwork is equal to it in any respect, with such proportion, beauty, and excellence. The craftsmanship is practically divine. But the implicit message is what's most particularly imposing on a psychological level.

Michelangelo carved *David* out of a six-ton rock, taking him three years to accomplish the feat. The realistic and highly detailed anatomy of the seventeen-foot tall statue make it a truly larger than life portrayal of David—*before* his battle with Goliath—armed with nothing but a sling in his hand.

We all know what happened next.

He slays the Philistine giant, then goes on to become king of Israel.

What does this mean for us?

In my estimation, *David,* and other works of art like it, can cull out our own *David,* in the form of a new invention, a company, a studio, a gym. Its sheer magnificence and what it represents beckons us to hearken the proclamation that, as Dr. Peterson's revelation suggested, we are not nearly what we could be.

I am not nearly what I could be is not synonymous with *I am not good enough.*

No way. They're not even in the same universe.

Which begs the question: who could you become if your new Default was *I am not nearly what I could be?*

Subway and The Way

March 27, 2023

I met with a local Pastor one night after visiting his church the first time the day before. If you look at the date, you might notice it was just hours after having my Epiphanal Moment.

After I told the Pastor what had transpired the past several months, he frowned, took off his glasses and said: "You're going to go undercover, under the radar," he said, wagging his glasses at me. "I don't know how and I don't know when, but you're going to be a minister in the marketplace."

Here's what happened in the following several months:

- Was jobless from then until September 8, 2023—the day I had an interview at the Subway down the road from our house.
- My first day as Sandwich Artist at Subway on September 10, 2023
- Promoted to Unit Manager on November 1, 2023
- Promoted to Multi-Unit Manager on April 3, 2024
- Promoted to District Manager on May 30, 2024

Yes, I've made thousands of sandwiches.

Yes, I handle labor and food costs.

Yes, I'm in charge of increasing sales and profitability at my stores.

But the majority of my job is, as Pastor predicted, ministry in the marketplace (though it masquerades as H.R. drama).

Here's the thing about some, not all, of the typical Subway employees. They're either:

- Minors whose Defaults are that of a victim, unable to turn life's adversities into their advantages.
- Adults who are stuck in self-sabotage, obviously, I was one of them. They're broken, victims to their own victimhood. They show up drunk to the job. They're late to clock-in. They're early to clock-out. They no-call, no-show on their last day because "What? It's my last day!" The irony in that statement hurts my head.

Well, now it all makes sense as to why God had me pursue extemporaneous speaking, doesn't it? I don't have time to prepare a speech when I'm on the job. My managers and employees ask me questions and bring me problems every day. I've got to come up with an answer or a solution, and fast. I can't yammer on and on, either. It's got to be simple and transparent, short and sweet, just like Table Topics.

In a way, I'm ministering to children and adults every single day, helping the former turn life's adversities into their advantages and the latter bridge the gap from self-sabotage to self-mastery. Overtime, they become better employees and better people.

But I do it in an undercover fashion, speaking to them in a way that sounds like H.R. instead of quoting scripture.

Get this. I sell *submarine* sandwiches. I'm *under* the radar. For me, at Subway, He is The Way. Subway is my undercover ministry.

This may be over-the-top, but it's my book so I'll define

it my way: whether you believe in Jesus Christ as your Lord and Savior is your business. Leaving relationships with Him aside, Subway taught me so much about myself. The lessons in humility alone are worth more than a lifetime supply of footlong sandwiches. Subway helped me grow up. Subway, in no small way, helped me finish this book.

In a way, Subway was The Way.

Why the 400?

I compete in all the sprint events, from as short as the sixty-meter dash, to as long—and dreadful—as the 400-meter. For those who are runners, this is going to sound strange—perhaps even masochistic—but the 400 is by far my favorite, and it's not even close.

Why?

To me, the 400-meter dash is a sixty-second hero's journey.

Think about it.

I finish where I start, blasting out of the starting blocks into the Extraordinary World.

After Crossing the First Threshold, around the 100-meter mark, I endure the Road of Trials; trying like hell to run *my* race instead of competing against the other runners to not wreck my pace, while simultaneously playing mental mind games with myself. *So far so good...This pace feels right, posture too...Nose-over-toes...Relax...Let go...Swing your arms—no—let your arms swing, just like that.*

As I lean into the second turn at 250 meters, I start feeling sorry for myself. Temptation makes me interrogate my reality. *Maybe I'm not in as good of shape as I thought?*

Then comes the All is Lost Moment. *This doesn't matter....This sucks...I can't win...It's just a stupid race...Who cares?* My upper back feels like a bundle of snakes as my muscles start to bind together, seemingly working against me. The lactic acid fills my calves first, then makes my ankles go from elastic to doughy, from springs to stumps.

Right when I want to quit is the time I turn the corner down the final 100 meters. The college kids standing in the infield chant my name.

"Let's go Hunter!"

"Sprint or die! C'mon Hunt!"

Then it hits me.

It's not about you, *Hunter.*

These kids don't give a damn if I win or take dead last—they're inspired. They see a dude in his thirties, weighing at least seventy pounds more than the competition, out here running against NCAA sprinters. They see a guy who decided he wasn't going to "hang it up" ten years prior; a guy who's scratching his own itch. That gives them hope, for themselves and for their future. The Epiphanal Moment.

I cross the finish line, reentering the Ordinary World. The kids I ran against pat my back, give me side-hugs, pound my fist with theirs.

"You're an inspiration, man."

A Gift for the People.

And now I'm sitting here using my gift of writing to tell the story. I'm a Master of Two Worlds. I'm an Artistic Warrior.

That's why the 400-meter dash is my favorite race, because it's not a race at all. It's a sixty-second hero's journey.

Scratch Your Own Itch—Part Two

May 5, 2023

When one journey ends, another begins.

Nearing the end of my hero's journey in Part Two, Kyle Galik and I were on a Zoom call. Not five minutes into our conversation, Avery and Alivia, my two nieces, had put on their *Little Stinker* hats and were wreaking havoc in the kitchen.

That meant Dad Duty.

Kyle set the phone down to go and restore order.

Meanwhile, as beguiling as the cedar ceiling in Kyle's garage was, I thumbed over to Instagram and began scrolling mindlessly to pass the time. I came across a post by the Green Bay Blizzard—Green Bay, Wisconsin's indoor football team.

I felt God's voice. He was calling me.

The Call to Adventure.

C'mon, I thought. *You can't be serious.*

"Sorry about that," Kyle said, picking up the phone.

"Hey," I said. "Would you ever play for the Blizzard?"

Kyle shook his head. "Nah," he said, the end of his cigar bloomed orange. "Too much risk of injury."

"Yeah," I said, frowning. "You're probably right. Sure would be a helluva lot of fun, though…"

Scratch Your Own Itch—Part Three

May 13, 2023

God didn't leave me alone about the football thing.

I went back and forth with Him on this for more than a week, wrestling with Him.

Maybe He was wrestling with *me?*

Refusal of the Call.

To hell with it, I thought, then got in touch with Derek, you remember him—the coach and mentor who helped me transform from powerlifter-to-sprinter.

I sent him a text:

> *Lmk your schedule in the coming days, weeks, or months…I'm sure you're busy and want to be respectful. No rush. I have something I want to 'run' by you, lol.*

May 15, 2023

Derek and I Zoomed shortly after noon. I posed the question to him about a guy like me, at my age, putting the pads on again.

"Well, you're certainly fit," he said, crossing his arms. "The training would be the easy part. We'd just have to work on the soft skills; see if someone would be willing to give you a chance."

"Yeah," I said, hanging my head and laughing. "I know it sounds stupid, but I know God put it on my mind and heart for a reason. At the same time, Derek, I'm in no rush. If it happens a year from now, great. If it happens a month from now, great."

Derek and I agreed to put out some feelers and to touch base in a week or so. After hanging up, I bowed my head and said: "God, this doesn't make any sense. I'm a sprinter. I'm thirty-two years old. I haven't played football in over ten years. I'm laying this at your feet. It's your problem now. If you want me to do this, then you need to make it obvious."

Famous last words.

My phone rang three hours later.

"Hey," it was Jay, a friend of mine. "Listen, don't know if this would be of any interest to you, but I just got off the phone with the owner of the RPFL. Ever heard of it?"

"Uhh, no."

"It's the Rivals Professional Football League," Jay said.

"Oh yeah?"

"They're a developmental league for the NFL. There's a tryout in Detroit on June thirtieth."

Supernatural Aid.

Hell, maybe I would be able to keep that promise I made to my dad?

There was only one way to find out.

I'd have to scratch my own itch.

When one journey ends, another begins.

Coda

On an episode of *Ask the 50 Billion Dollar Man,* Mr. Peña was asked the question:

"Has QLA ever worked for an *author?"*

"No," Mr. Peña said. "Next."

November 30, 2023

I'm at my desk, doing what I do best.

I've gone all-in on writing, baby.

I have my Dream Team in place. My editor, David, and my literary agent, Sharon.

They're good at what they do, very good. Not just because they saw the potential this book had, because they brought out the best in me. And to my utter amazement, both were gracious enough to work with me on a success fee basis.

Can you believe that?

I guess you could say that meant they believed in me.

It also meant they believed in you.

So did I.

Without you, what the hell's the point?

I'm getting ahead of myself now. The book has been pitched to several publishers. Now we wait.

A deal could be days away.

May 31, 2024

One day after being promoted to District Manager at Subway, I got an email from my agent.

The subject line read: Woohoo - We've Received a Contract Offer!

Winged Publications and I agreed to terms.

I got my first deal done, and it didn't cost me a dime. I have to pinch myself multiple times throughout the day to believe it, but it's true: I am the first mentee to make QLA work as an author.

To Mr. Peña I say, thank you. I look forward to seeing you again real soon.

And thanks to you too, for taking the time out of your busy schedule to read this book.

Speaking of books, I've got to get going on the sequel. It's begging to be written. I've got to scratch my own itch. As for this one? It's done. It's not perfect, and I'm okay with that. Done is better than perfect. If I kept on writing, it'd be self-sabotage. It's behind me now. It is finished.

And besides, I can't rewrite what's already been written, but I can start a new chapter…*today*.

Won't you do the same?

THE END

ABOUT THE AUTHOR

Hunter Charneski is the District Manager of Grand Rapids for Empire Hospitality Group, overseeing several Subway restaurants in West Michigan. He still competes at NCAA meets in the sixty, 100, 200, and 400-meter dashes. When he isn't working, writing, or competing, he is playing *Destiny* online with his son, Sam. He lives in Georgetown Township, Michigan, with his wife, Tiffany Charneski, and their three cats, Toulouse, Navy, and Clarence.

www.ingramcontent.com/pod-product-compliance
Lightning Source LLC
Chambersburg PA
CBHW061132120626
46546CB00005B/1749
9781965352144